RECIPES FROM AN
UNKNOWN KITCHEN

by Rita Godfrey

Refried Books

Published by Fitzalan Publishers
www.fitzalanpublishers.co.uk

ISBN – 978-0-9576961-1-2
A catalogue record of this book is available
from the British Library

www.refriedbooks.co.uk

A big thank you to all those friends who lent me their
crockery, taste buds and opinions.
It wouldn't be the same without you.

And the biggest thank you to Debbie Kennedy
of norobotshere, without whom this
book wouldn't have happened.

Introduction

And Welcome

How many of us have scribbled down a recipe from a book, from our family or from a friend?

Have you jotted down a recipe heard on the radio? Do you keep a notebook especially for written recipes - or pop them in the back of a favourite recipe book or on an envelope tucked in between books on the shelf?

Who will find these recipes when we have passed on the book or passed on ourselves? What will they make of our lives?

I have a book on my shelf called *My Treasured Recipes* in which I have written down my favourite recipes. I revisit this and use it often, and I have included a couple of them in this book.

I have a job I absolutely love, buying and selling old cookery and gardening books. As *Refried Books* I come across some wonderful books, including those I have real trouble selling on. In some, previous owners have made their mark, adding comments as they find a better way of cooking or changing quantities, adding ingredients and making the recipes their own. To purists, these scribbles and jottings reduce the value of the book, but to me, knowing that some other cook has held that book or propped it up while they read through the recipe makes it even more valuable. Perhaps they were preparing a meal for a special occasion, a new cook trying something for the first time or a seasoned cook trying yet another recipe to avoid mid-week boredom by using a new ingredient or finding a new way to use a familiar ingredient.

As I open the pages I can see which recipes were the favourites, with fingerprints and creases, grease marks, bright colours from a bit of turmeric or beetroot, a splodge of gravy or pesto. I feel I know that cook a bit better and we have something in common. These are real books used by real people - as I'm sure every author hoped they would be.

I also come across the absolute delight that is a hand-written recipe book. Who wrote these, took the time to sit down and make a permanent record of their favourites and why? Some have a name in or a date; sometimes they are in another language, or two or three. Some are so old that the language and ingredients are unfamiliar.

I decided to gather together some of these private records and bring them out into the light to a new audience so that their authors are remembered and the recipes can have another life.

I have also tried where I can to give some kind of the background to the times these were written in and to describe the type of ingredients, cooking utensils and social background at the time.

What Do People Write Down?

Everything, although there seems to be a disproportionate number of cake and biscuit recipes. In choosing which recipes to include - and there are hundreds - I have tried to mix classic dishes of the day with some surprises, things I had never heard of.

It has been a hard job paring them down to give you a taste of what these cooks have

recorded, but I have enjoyed every minute. And I hope you will grow to love these unknown cooks in unknown kitchens as much I do.

Weights and Measures

The measures given in the recipes vary from 'take some flour' through a dram to a gill to pounds, ounces, kilograms and grams, including cups, pints, quarts and litres on the way - even stones in one recipe!

So in translating and trying the recipes I have used spoons, grams and mls. Of course being an inconsistent soul, there are occasions where cups have been the best measure. I hope it all makes sense.

Eggs used are all medium except where specified and milk is semi-skimmed.

In translating I have made some slight changes to reflect modern tastes, I have reduced salt, sugar and fats from some recipes. Cooking times have been changed as well to reflect the speedy cooking times of modern appliances; one of the benefits given for the gas ranges introduced in the early 20th century was that you could boil a kettle in 15 minutes! It just shows how cooking times have changed.

And methods, where possible I have used time-saving methods such as food processors, blenders and microwave cooking, so much easier!

Recipe Sources

The sources of the recipes I have included vary from neat, indexed, hand-written recipe books, to recipe books half hand-written and full of cutouts from magazines, to scribbled notes on just about anything that has come to the cook's hand from telephone note pages to the back of envelopes. They also include recipes that have been written on the pages of printed recipe books.

With all of these wonderful books, the problem has been choosing which recipes out of the hundreds to use but along the way I have found recipes which have become firm favourites.

You can never really be sure, unless someone has dated each recipe exactly, in what year the notes start and end, especially as most of them seemed to have been passed down from person to person, cook to cook. A recipe I found in one of the

books, with the name F. Ciatio has a recipe for China Chilo, this recipe is also in another book I found which did have a date of 1742 to 1836. I then found the recipe absolutely word for word in *A New System Of Domestic Cookery* (1807) by Maria Eliza Ketelby Rundell. So who wrote it first and when?

The older recipes come from the more formal recipe books - paper was a expensive and a notebook was a valuable item.

1821

A beautiful and fragile leather bound book with the inscription *W. Sayer, His Book, 1821*. The recipes are beautifully written, indexed and neat. The writing covers every centimeter of the pages and the last third or so has been taken over by another author - they didn't throw books away then.

It is likely that William was a chef in a wealthy household. The ingredients are often expensive using the best cuts and the quantities are large. The very first page has the recipe for **Pineapple Ice**, one that I've included in this book, and pineapples didn't come cheap, having been grown in a hothouse.

It is from this book that the recipes for **Oxford Sausages** come with a footnote – *Lucens/ Lacens College Oxford Mr Bickman*, although I can't find any reference to this college.

But William doesn't only include recipes for food. In a time when each household had to make everything from scratch he also records, amongst others, recipes for Lady Derby's soap, cold cream, pomade, a recipe for a severe cough, Burton Ale, homemade wines and a patent method for preserving eggs. The recipe for **Curaçao, Goffres à la Hollondaise, Camp Vinegar** and **Currie Powder** also came from this book.

Recipes tried and rejected from William's book are Damson Cakes (I couldn't get the texture right but I am still trying) and Hunters Beef (I couldn't get the saltpeter for the brine).

1850s

The second is a coverless section of a book, the main block of which has survived. It includes a lot more day-to-day recipes than William's book but still aims for quality. Was the writer a housekeeper or lady of the house? I get the sense of a book

used regularly and there are spots and marks from cooking. The handwriting looks like that of a woman and is fine and neat.

Recipes I included from this volume include **A Harico Mutton** and **Cream Flummery** both using expensive ingredients - this was a household that ate well.

As with William's book it includes recipes for household stuffs including blacking, black ink and hart's horn jelly (used to treat diahorrea). There are remedies for whooping cough and colic amongst other ailments and instructions on how to save a barrel of beer that has gone sour - an important recipe in a time when people drank beer rather than water and most country houses brewed their own.

It was calculated that in1800 about half the production of beer was domestic. The tradition of home brewing in farms and cottages was an almost universal feature of country life, both beer and homemade wines.

Tried and rejected from this slim volume are Soused Pigs Feet and Ears, as the texture of the ears made my teeth vibrate.

A little document also from this period, the main part an index from a recipe book gave me the recipe for **Cherry Marmalade**. The tiny writing has squeezed as much on to each page as possible.

1911-1930s

A household accounts book written by Mrs Berry with an address in Tunbridge Wells and dated December 1911 (presumably the start date). Lots of the recipes in it are attributed to Mother or E Shepherd. This book has lots of basic recipes – roast beef, rabbit pie, Yorkshire pudding, how to cook vegetables, pastries and sauces. I think this might be the notebook of a new wife, calling on the knowledge of her mother and friends.

The ingredients lead me to believe that she is probably middle class; although they are not extravagant, they do include good cuts of meat - roast beef wasn't generally part of a working man's diet – and she used good steak for her steak pie. On the other hand, the book does include recipes

for beef and cow heel, so there is some need for economy. It also contains recipes for other household needs: eye lotion, Aunt Alice's blood mixture. Has anyone heard of Zambuck, which includes 'oil of swallows'?

In fact Mrs Berry's book was so packed full of recipes I could have written a book just including her. Very organised, unlike me, she also includes a list of birthdays for the family and at the end a few knitting patterns and addresses of family and friends (one of which has the date 1930). This book is where I found **Mock Mango Chutney, Potted Meat Paste, Spion Cops, Blackberries Pudding** and **Fish Pastry**.

1898-1933

The next is a notebook which spans from 1898 (there is a list of biscuits cooked for Christmas 1898) to around 1930s (there are a couple of recipes with the notation of 1933). The cover is damaged and beaten up through years of storage and damp but the pages are easily readable. Indexed, the book looks as though it was intended as an address book, and is full of recipes on scraps of paper. This is a gold mine of information and appears to be the notebook of a cook or housekeeper, full of both basic and more 'gourmet' recipes such as sautéed chicken à la Morengo, lobster cutlets, and oyster soup.

This book was so full of recipes I had a hard time choosing which to use. Some recipes not included, are Aunt Kate's Pudding, Fennel sauce for Mackerel and Bermuda Stacks. Rejected were A Warming Drink (that really just tasted of peppermint oil and sugar) and Sheep Head Pie.

It was in this book that I found **Kromskies, Salad Cream, Kedgeree, Green Pea Soup, Giblet Soup, Blackberry Vinegar,** and **Coffee Cream.**

I also have a diary of meals cooked from Nov 1897 to March 1889 which was with this recipe book. It lists both menus for family meals and for occasions aimed, I assume, at making sure that guests weren't given the same food twice and that the family had a varied diet.

1903 – 1930

A copy of *The Samaritan Cookbook* has blank pages for the users notes and Lucy Brown has made the most of these -

they are full of added recipes. The book was published in 1903 in aid of The Glasgow Hospital for Women. In itself it is a lovely cookery book and quite hard to find. But this copy has been personalised by Lucy.

The book is full of advertisements for local traders and includes one for Findlay's Perfection Range - a marvellous edifice of iron, probably similar to one Lucy cooked on. Some of the recipes are dated and the latest one is dated 1939 (Apricot Jam).

Most of the recipes seem to come from friends, such as Jenny's Pudding, A. Burton's Wheaten Loaf and Mrs Smith's Ginger Nuts. She was obviously an avid cook - the book has been well used - and she seems to have been a collector of recipes (including a large number of scone and jam recipes).

Again these include recipes for household stuffs – recipe for a stained ceiling, how to clean dirty hands. I think I like Lucy.

From her notes I included **Spiced Treacle Scones, Batchelor Cake** and **Mrs Smith's Ginger Nuts.**

I can see which recipes were the favourites, with fingerprints and creases, grease marks, bright colours from a bit of turmeric or beetroot, a splodge of gravy or pesto...

I wanted to make the Inglenook Toffee but couldn't read her tiny writing on this page.

One hand-written book of recipes, *Kochrecepts*, begins with recipes written in German, then changes to French then to English. Alongside the English recipes are newspaper cuttings by food writers Pearl Adam, Ambrose Heath and Countess Morphy, all who wrote columns (and books) from the late 20s and through the 30s, helping to date it.

I think I will have to go back to the German recipes at some point; the handwriting is beautiful, much better than the English handwriting later. Was it brought over from Germany and passed on through the family? There are no clues, but I would like to think so.

This book was predominantly recipes for cakes, biscuits and sweet things but I had to winnow out a just a few of those which was really difficult. Included from Kochrecepts are **Mysterious Pudding** and **Bishops Bread**.

1942-1948

One lovely notebook has a few newspaper cuttings (strangely, nearly all for marrow and ginger jam), which have articles on the reverse that date from 1942 – 1948. It has a name in pencil in the front - F. Ciatio, I think (the writing is hard to read.) I think it may have been started before then as the recipes in the front of the book and the handwriting is earlier than on the pages with the news cuttings.

As with previous books, the handwriting changes as the book has been handed on or handed down. Most of the recipes are for day-to-day food, which is nice to see, with a section on meatless dishes of which I have included **Cheese Pudding** and **Irish Potatoes Pudding.**

I chose quite a few recipes from this book including **Patriotic Pudding, Egg Pie, Indian Trifle, Blackberry Jelly, Potato Bread and Casserole of Lettuce.** Although some I haven't included are those which time does not improve such as Sheep's Head and Livers and Eel Pie.

Surprisingly, the recipes aren't tailored for lack of ingredients through rationing, so there's no dried egg, not a lot of margarine and sugar seems to be used quite liberally.

In addition to the food recipes were other household recipes including (I kid you not) `A Remedy for Diptheria!'

1950s

G. R. Moore, with an address in Rotherham and a date of 1955, half-filled a notebook with neat recipes. Laid out very neatly, this could be the notebook of someone who was learning to cook; the layout looks more like a school or college book than a kitchen book and the writing looks quite young.

Most of the recipes have huge gaps in the methods, so either he/ she thought they would remember how to cook these but needed to be reminded of the ingredients or was lazy and didn't bother more than he/she needed to!

The recipes are quite basic and most are for baking. The recipes for **Harvo** and **Fidget Pie** come from this book. Missing - but I'm still trying! - is Jap Cakes, that stable of the British Bakers in the 1950s, I will get it right one day.

1940s-1960s

A fabulous find was G. Watson's book. Crammed with recipes and marked through with smudges and grease marks, this is a book that has been used well.

This book covers a period from 1940s to 1960s with dated recipes from 1948. There are recipes for food cooked with rationed ingredients including lots of dried egg, a few marked 'from the TV' and one 'from Philip Harben', one of the first TV chefs who was on television from 1946 through the fifties and sixties.

This book also had lots of Hungarian recipes - was G. Watson of Hungarian descent? From here I included **Wartime Chutney, Elderberry Ketchup, Betty's Chocolate Spread** and **Salade Fifi.**

In the back of the book is this great exercise routine :

Stretch to the ceiling /Stretch to the floor
Swing to the window /Swing to the door
Bend by the table / Foot on the chair
Head on your knee and Stretch in the air.
I do love these books.

1980s

Chloe's book is dated 1984 and marked *Vol III*, so Chloe was a great collector of recipes.

Here is a book half-written but with a lot of the recipes ascribed to well-known cooks and chefs. I haven't included these; rather I have chosen those which look as though they have been passed on by friends and family.

In a way Chloe's book reflects how recipes were passed on by the 1980s. Gone were the days when new cooks learned from 'mother.' Instead the television cooks and their books brought new and up-to-date recipes – after all, who wants to eat old-fashioned foods?

She has also used the book to note special dates and on the back page there are various notes including *'December 27th 1983 – girl canary laid her first egg while we were off to Birdworld.'* *'Slim's daughter born 2nd Jan 1984 – Sophie'.* *'Jan 7th 1984 first walk in space'.*

The last note refers to the news that on Feb. 7, 1984, two Challenger space shuttle astronauts, Capt. Bruce McCandless II and Col. Robert L. Stewart, performed the first untethered spacewalk during the STS-41B mission. *'Free of any lifeline and propelled into the dark void by tiny jets, they became, in effect, the first human satellites.'*

From Chloe's book I have used **Crema Catalan**.

1980s-2000

The next book is anonymous and full of snippets from newspapers and magazines. An envelope with a recipe and a newspaper cutting have the dates 1995 & 1996 & 2003.

There are masses of small snips of paper with recipes. Whoever this was dashed down recipes on anything to hand – from the television or radio perhaps? The book is full - here is someone who loved to try new things.

Lots of the recipes have been passed on from friends and there are lots of recipes from Dick, Mary and Hilary. I love this book; it looks like the sort of untidy collection of recipes I have.

From here I have used **Mary's Quince Jelly, Peaches in Burgundy, Tarte Au Pizza à La Jacqueline, Jacqueline Boeuf** au Vin, **Hil's Soup** and **Ginger Nut and Whipped Cream Desert**.

My Treasured Recipes published in the 80s is a book designed for recording recipes and two recipes came from here – **Salade Pêcheur** (the results of French holidays) and **Elderflower Cordial**, the last recipe of all dated 1999 (Clarice's recipe).

And the others...

Other recipes come from a series of scraps of paper found in the pages of cookery books.

The first were in a copy of *Mrs Beeton's Everyday Cooking* published in 1907. Whoever wrote these was either in a hurry or used to reading her own shorthand and we have to fill in the gaps where she has assumed she will remember the rest of the instruction or quantities. A housewife who didn't have to share the recipes. Onion porridge – strangely nice.

Vin d'Oranges and **Soupe au Pistou** from a note found in *Simca's Cuisine* - a great book on French cooking from the 60s.

The Queen's Recipe Barley Water written in the back of

Natural Folk Recipes, published in the 1970s.

Carrot Cake from a note slipped into a book dated 1970 along with **Arabella's Cheesecake**. Both of these typewritten rather than handwritten.

My Colannon from a note written on a telephone message pad.

And from lots of hand written notes, one recipe which is not from an unknown kitchen – my mum's recipe for **Melting Moments**. I had to include it, although why she had it written down I don't know - I'm pretty sure she knew this one by heart. Mum was an excellent cook and did all her own baking in the 50s and 60s on a Rayburn.

As the century went on there are less handwritten recipe books, perhaps because recipes from cookery books were more available or TV chefs started to take over with new and exciting recipes where old family favourites fell out of favour. Also, I hope, the cooks of the 70s, 80s and 90s are still cooking and using their notebooks!

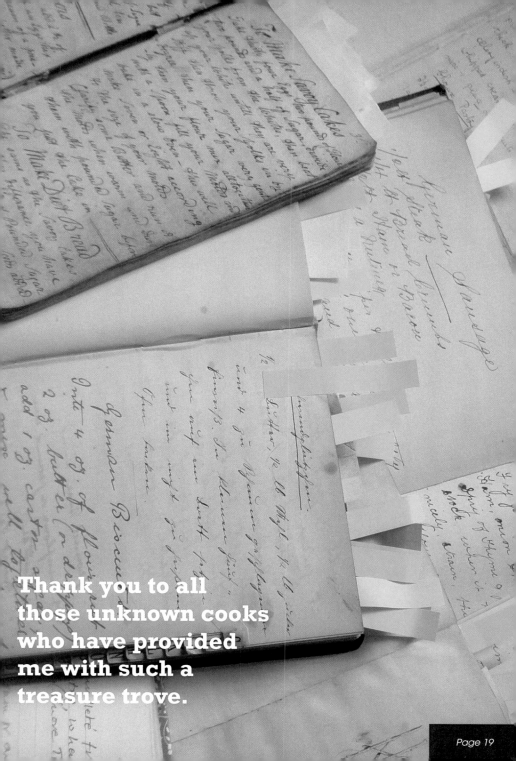

Thank you to all those unknown cooks who have provided me with such a treasure trove.

Contents
1800-1950

1800-1900

1900-1930

1930-1950

Contents
1950-2000

1950-1980

1980-2000

1800 – 1900

The Recipes

1800-1900

The History

The Background

The 1800s were marked by vast industrial development, by factories and gadgets, extravagance and pollution, mass poverty and charity and an age of mechanisation brought by coal and steam.

The century opened with the Napoleonic wars which ended with Waterloo in 1815. George Washington became the 1st president of USA, the Bastille fell in Paris, the Act of the Union was raised in Ireland in 1800. So - lots of change.

In Britain, country life was plagued by poor harvests and crop disease, leading to famine and food riots. Female literacy rates in 1851 were still only 55% compared to nearly 70% for men. So handwritten recipe books were generally the product of the upper classes or housekeepers and chefs to the rich and the recipes I have here reflect the extravagance of the ingredients. These were not the recipes of the poor!

The Kitchen

Domestic labour was cheap and this allowed for lavish eating styles of the prosperous and the time consuming preparation of food. With all these servants, the invention of kitchen equipment for every element of food preparation could be made as complicated as you like and the Victorian kitchen inventors brought out a utensil, pan or implement for every job - all needing cleaning of course. For most of the 1800s, although in the country they were still using open fires, urban dwellers used kitchen ranges fed by wood and coal fuel and these great iron behemoths needed constant attention. At the end of the century domestic gas ovens were available, promoted by the forward-thinking chef Alexis Soyer, although not much used.

In 1856, pasturisation was invented in France by Louis Pasteur, a great step forward in health and food preservation. Foods needed to be preserved to keep through the winter and the 'mean months' of the spring until new crops were available. Despite better transport - Macadam had invented the road covering and rail was common - and the invention of canning, preserving was still a necessity rather than a 'hobby' as it is today.

During the 18th century, sugar became enormously popular. Britain, for example, consumed five times as much sugar in 1770 as in 1710. By 1750 sugar surpassed grain as 'the most valuable commodity in European trade.' As Europeans established sugar plantations on the larger Caribbean islands, prices fell, especially in Britain. By the 18th century all levels of society had become common consumers of the former luxury product.

At first most sugar in Britain went into hot drinks, but later confectionery and chocolates became extremely popular. Many Britons (especially children) also ate jams. Sweet recipes were collected and shared.

In most households, fresh meat was a luxury seen only on Sunday when there might be enough meat for a pudding or 'toad' encased in suet crust. However in the country there was always wild meat - rabbits, pigeons - which meant the country cook generally had a better diet than the town cook. More of the animal was eaten - I found a recipes for sheep's trotter in one

manuscript. Of course, the upper classes weren't affected by any of this.

The invention in the late 17th century of a muslin cloth for steaming fed England's obsession with puddings - previously, a cook would have had to obtain fresh animal guts in which to steam her pudding. And the English had an enormous appetite for puddings, whether stuffed with meat or game, or oozing with butter or custard.

Tunbridge Water Cakes

William Sayer

I have seen references to these biscuits called *Tunbridge Wafers* or *Romary Biscuits* after the baker Alfred Romary who had a bakery in Tunbridge, opened in 1862.

Romary later received Royal warrants for his wafers. Recipes seem to vary of course - some versions are more savoury and this writer has added orange flower water.

Ingredients

250g butter

250g icing sugar

500g flour

3 egg yolks

1 tablespoon orange flower water

Method

Preheat the oven to 180°C/350°F/Gas 4.

Rub the butter in with the flour. Add the sugar and make the whole into a paste.

Don't work too much as this will make the biscuits hard. Roll out very thinly on a floured table and cut out with a plain round or scalloped cutter about 3" across.

Place them on a greased baking tray and bake them to a pale delicate colour.

They take about 15 – 20 minutes depending on your oven.

These make lovely biscuits for children to decorate. This mix makes about fifty biscuits.

Soda Cake

Anon

Although we don't know the name of the writer, he or she has noted that this is 'Mrs Baker's Recipe'

Soda cake uses baking soda to help it rise. Self-raising flour incorporating baking powder was invented by Henry Jones and patented in 1845, so before that using baking soda was the norm. A good staple cake, nice with a cup of tea.

Ingredients

750g plain flour

175g butter

250g caster sugar

250g currants

1 teaspoon baking soda

3 eggs

150ml milk

10 drops lemon essence

Juice of ½ lemon

Pinch of salt

Method

Preheat the oven to 180°C/350°F/Gas 4.

Mix all the ingredients in a food processor. You may need a little more milk until it is at a stiff dropping consistency (as my old Home Economics teacher would say).

Spoon it into an 8" (20cm) round cake tin, preferably a springform, that has been greased.

After 50 minutes test with a skewer to make sure it is cooked - it may need up to an hour

You may need to cover the top with foil if it needs longer, to prevent it going too brown.

A good staple cake, nice with a cup of tea.

Goffres à la Hollondoise

William Sayer

These lovely little waffles were introduced by the French, although the name of this recipe would suggest William got the recipe via Holland. In Belgium the spelling is *Gauffres* where they are a traditional dessert with many different types of waffles.

Of those, two are particularly well-known. One is Brussels Waffles (*Gaufre de Bruxelles*), made from batter leavened with beaten eggs. It is served with powdered sugar (aka icing/confectioner's sugar.) As the formed waffles cook on the griddle, the sugar melts and caramelises on the outside of the waffle

Anyway they are delicious! Especially with maple syrup, fruit purée or cooked, tart fruit such as blackcurrants (with squirty cream.)

Ingredients

2 eggs

100g caster sugar

100g butter

100g plain flour

100ml milk

1 tablespoonful orange flower water

Grated peel of a lemon

Method

Beat together the eggs and sugar, followed by the butter, flour then milk. Mix well. (Actually it doesn't matter if it is a bit lumpy it comes out in the cooking). Then finally add the orange flower water and lemon zest.

These can be cooked either in a waffle maker, on a waffle iron or as little pancakes on a griddle or frying pan - but don't add any oil to cook. They just take a few minutes

When they are dark golden, put them on a rack for a moment or two to crisp up. They stay crisp for quite a while.

Don't make too many, you won't be able to stop eating them.

A Harico Mutton

Anon

A ragout made with hashed mutton and turnips. In old French, *harigot, harligot,* and *haligote* are all found, meaning a morsel or a piece.

Versions of this recipe have been found dating back to 1600. It is a common recipe of the time for the poor as well as the better-off. Some new recipes mistakenly add haricot beans assuming the name comes from these.

This is deceptively tasty for so simple a dish.

Ingredients

500g mutton (use best end of neck, leg or shoulder) chopped into small pieces or 1 cm slices)

2 tablespoons olive oil

1 pint lamb stock

A sprig each of thyme and rosemary

A small bay leaf

2 blades of mace

pepper & salt

4 carrots, peeled and diced

A small turnip peeled and diced

1 large onion, peeled and sliced

1 rounded tablespoon flour

Method

Heat the oil in a thick-bottomed saucepan and fry the sliced onions and pieces of meat for a few minutes until browned. Stir in the flour and cook gently for about 5 minutes, stirring all the time.

Add the carrots, turnip, herbs and seasoning.

Cover and simmer gently for about 2 hours.This recipe can also be adapted for lamb, in which case it only needs to be simmered for about an hour.

Taste and season if necessary.

Best served with mashed potato - I have also used parsnip instead of turnip.

Oxford Sausages

William Sayer

The first published reference to a sausage that closely resembles the modern Oxford sausage is by John Nott in his book The Cook's and Confectioner's Dictionary: Or, the Accomplish'd Housewife's Companion, published in London in 1723. Traditionally, Oxford sausages are noted for the addition of veal, in contrast to many traditional British sausages which contain only pork, and their high level of spice seasoning.

References to the 'Oxford' style of sausage date back to at least the early 18th century, but it was more widely popularised owing to inclusion in Mrs Beeton's *Book of Household Management*, first published in 1861.

William puts two versions of Oxford Sausages in his book. Both recipes have the note 'Mr Bickman' as a reference. I wonder who he was?

This recipe doesn't call for the high spicing of the sausage found in other recipes.

Both recipes have the note 'Mr Bickman' as a reference. I wonder who he was..?

As first produced, the Oxford sausage did not have a skin or other casing, but was hand-formed and floured before frying. However, modern forms are commonly made in a conventional, linked banger style, with natural pork or sheep casng.

Neither of these recipes use flour for frying.

I have combined the two recipes and modernised them by removing the suet which was in the recipe at the same quantity as the veal.

Ingredients

1 kg leg of pork
500g lean veal
100g slightly stale bread
3 eggs, beaten
1 tablespoon chopped sage
1 teaspoon salt
½ teaspoon ground black pepper
½ teaspoon ground nutmeg
½ teaspoon ground mace
Oil or butter for frying

Method

Mince the pork and veal.

Add the bread to the beaten egg.

Mix all the ingredients together well. The sausage mix can be prepared a day before you roll out the sausages and kept in the fridge to bring out the flavour of the sage and spices.

Roll the sausages about the size of your finger.

Keep them constantly stirring over a high heat and when brown, test. Modern recipes also add finely ground lemon rind which adds a bit of zing.

Chicken Fricassée

Anon

A fricassée is halfway between a sauté and a stew.

A true classic, with as many variations as there are grandmothers in France, it relies on humble ingredients and just a single pot. It's the original French comfort food: simmered chicken in a rich, silky sauce.

This early version leaves out the sauté step and the result is lovely and moist.

Ingredients

4 skinned chicken joints

600ml milk

½ teaspoon nutmeg

3 pieces mace

½ teaspoon salt

¼ teaspoon pepper

A sprig of tarragon

An onion cut in half

25g flour

25g butter

50 ml single cream

A squeeze of lemon juice

Method

Use a heavy-bottomed pan.

Place the chicken pieces in the pan and add the milk, spices, herbs and the onion. You may need more milk depending on the size of your pan - you want to cover the meat.

Heat until it is just boiling and simmer very, very gently until the meat is well cooked; about 30 – 40 minutes depending on the size of the joints of meat. If you want to speed things up, you can cut the meat into smaller pieces, but not into bite-sized pieces as it is better from the bone.

Remove from the pan. Mix the butter and flour and beat into a little of the milk, then add this to the pan to thicken.

Add the cream and lemon juice, taste and add seasoning if needed.

A true classic, with as many variations as there are grandmothers in France...

Collige Pudding

Anon

An early spelling of the *College Pudding*, a traditional pudding served to students in the halls of Oxford and Cambridge.

Nearly every Oxford and Cambridge college has a slightly different pudding named after it. This version has the addition of brandy and white wine and that, with the nutmeg, gives a nice spicy flavour.

Ingredients

150g suet
150g breadcrumbs
150g currants and candied peel
120g soft brown sugar
1 tablespoon brandy
1 tablespoon white wine
A good grating of nutmeg
2 whole eggs
2 egg yolks
Milk

Method

Mix all of the dry ingredients together.

Beat the egg and add to the dry ingredients with enough of the milk to produce a soft dropping consistency - the amount depends on how fresh the breadcrumbs are. Add the brandy and white wine.

Spoon into a greased 2 pint (1.1 litre) pudding basin, cover securely and steam for 2 hours.

This pudding turns out easily if left for a few minutes after taking it out of the steamer.

Turn out and serve with custard.

Nearly every Oxford and Cambridge college has a slightly different pudding named after it.

I don't know how these are pronounced - Nice puddings or nice puddings?

Little Nice Puddings

William Sayer

Again, a very sweet little dish, a sugary egg custard using just the whites of eggs. It is rather like a cross between a soufflé and a Crème brûlée.

Ingrediients

Whites of 7 eggs
60ml single cream
125g butter (melted)
125g icing sugar
60g plain flour

Method

Preheat the oven to 180°C/350°F/Gas 4.

Whisk egg whites until fairly stiff.

Take the cream and add the melted butter, then fold in the flour little by little.

Add the egg whites and the sugar and mix well.

Pour the mix into greased ramekin dishes.

Cook in a bain marie or a roasting dish with a little water in the bottom for 35 minutes or until the top has risen and is a golden brown.

They will drop as soon as they come out of the oven and won't look as pretty, but they taste good.

These go well with something tart such as raspberry coulis or cooked blackcurrants.

Pine Apple Ice

William Sayer

In the 1800s, to have ice in the summer was a sign of wealth. Large estates may have had their own ice houses.

In England, ice was imported into England from Norway on a considerable scale. Either they saved it in insulated ice houses in the winter, by storing it in underground ice stores (you can see one at Scotney castle in Kent) or if they lived near high mountains, they brought great chunks of the stuff down in the summer.

In America, the ice trade, also known as the frozen water trade, was a 19th century industry, centering on the east coast of the United States and Norway. Ice was cut from the surface of ponds and streams, then stored in ice houses, before being sent on by ship, barge or railway to its final destination around the world.

The marketing in the later 19th century of *Mrs Marshall's Patent Freezer* was a revelation, a hand-cranked machine that used a mixture of ice and salt to freeze, claiming to make ice cream in 3 minutes. Mrs Marshall's book on ices is a classic, and still a much sought-after book.

Ingredients

A small pineapple
(about 300g of flesh when peeled)
One lemon
400ml single cream
100ml pineapple juice
150g castor sugar

Method

Pulp the flesh of the pineapple in a food processor on pulse. This doesn't want to be puréed, just reduced to small lumps.

If using an ice cream maker, add the pineapple juice, sugar and lemon juice directly to the machine. While they are mixing, add the cream. When the mix has frozen and thickened, store in a container in the freezer.

If you are mixing by hand, put them all in a bowl and mix, then transfer to a container and put in the freezer compartment. After one hour, mix with a fork to break up the lumps, then repeat an hour later.

This is not a soft-scoop ice cream, so take it out of the freezer around 20 minutes before serving. The result should be halfway between a sorbet and ice cream.

Cream Flummery

Anon

Flummery was popular from the 17th to the 19th century.

The origin of the word is obscure. It might derive from the similar Welsh dish *llymru*. But as *llummery* can also mean 'empty nonsense,' the name may equally derive from the custom of giving end-of-meal sweetmeats some sort of slightly comic title to indicate an unimportant or trivial thing, as is the probable derivation of 'flan', 'trifle' and 'fool'.

This recipe is quite an upmarket version.

Ingredients

600ml cream

1 teaspoon cornflour
(mix with a little of the cream)

75g sugar

50g almonds, beaten with a spoonful of milk

Whites of 3 eggs beaten to a soft peak

Method

Add the eggs, cream, sugar and cornflour to the almonds in a thick-bottomed pan over a medium heat.

Bring to the boil slowly, stirring all the time, until it thickens to the consistency of custard.

Take off the heat and pour into individual glasses. Cool, then store in the fridge until needed.

You can add flavours such as vanilla, cinnamon or chocolate to the mixture before heating, but I like it as it is.

You can add flavours such as vanilla, cinnamon or chocolate to the mixture...

Dutch Pickle

William Sayer

An early version of pickle, similar to piccalilli. In 1758, Hannah Glasse described 'how to make Paco-Lilla, or India Pickle.' This is slightly different in that it doesn't include the turmeric that gives piccalilli its defining colour, but does include horseradish, which gives it a real bite.

Ingredients

1 head of cauliflower

1 white cabbage

500g small onions

150g salt

10g horseradish (peeled and finely chopped)

1 large clove garlic (skinned and thinly sliced)

1 tablespoon dry English mustard

1.5 litres of wine vinegar

Spices for vinegar

1 tablespoon whole cloves

6 peppercorns

1 small bay leaf

2 blades mace

1 stick cinnamon, about 10 cm

Method

Chop the cauliflower and white cabbage into small pieces and put them into a bowl. Add the small onions and pour boiling water over them with the salt. Stand for twelve hours, then drain, rinse and dry them.

Add the spices to the vinegar in a saucepan.

Bring to the boil and let it stand for 1–2 hours. You can prepare this at the same time as the vegetables and leave overnight.

Mix the garlic, horseradish and mustard with the vinegar. Bring it to the boil and strain it through double muslin onto the vegetables.

Transfer to sealed, vinegar-proof jars and label. This pickle is never very clear as the horseradish and mustard make it a little cloudy, but that doesn't affect the flavour.

Camp Vinegar
(shake before use)

Camp Vinegar

William Sayer

Soy sauce has been used in Asia for hundreds of years. India Soy was a later addition; the first soyfood product, *Fine India Soy* was sold in Sydney in 1804.

Indian-style soy sauce varies from Chinese by the addition of chillies. It is quite hard to find but is available by internet.

The recipe calls for colouring but I have left it out in the modernised version of this vinegar.

This is hot and very garlicky and one of those very adaptable ingredients, an early version of Worcestershire Sauce but not so sweet. I have used it in casseroles, on cheese on toast and in salad dressings.

Ingredients

1 large bulb of garlic

15g cayenne pepper

2 tablespoons India soy

4 anchovies (chopped)

600ml of good white wine vinegar

Method

Take a large head of garlic and cut it into slices. Add cayenne pepper, the India Soy and anchovies. If you can't find India Soy, use light soy sauce and up the cayenne a little (but not too much).

Put all of these into the white wine vinegar in a large sealed jar. Leave for about six weeks shaking it often, then pour it through double muslin to clear Store in vinegar-proof bottles.

Indian-style soy sauce varies from Chinese by the addition of chillies

Mushroom Catsup

Anon

Catsup or ketchup is a condiment based on just about anything.

The origin of the word is said to date to 17th century China, where a spicy pickled fish sauce was called *ke-tsiap,* meaning 'brine of pickled fish or shellfish'.

It was first introduced to the West by seamen returning from voyages to the Far East, and arrived in England where it evolved in many directions with the addition of anything from mangoes to walnuts to mushrooms, eventually becoming the tomato sauce we know so well.

Nowadays most recipes include vinegar, but this one uses beer which gives it a less sharp but interesting flavour. The recipe called for stale beer but unfortunately I only had fresh.

I used flat mushrooms which I think give a better flavour but they do give it a dark colour and make it look a little like henna. Commercial mushrooms would make a lighter sauce and I have seen versions using dried mushrooms.

Ingredients

2.5 litres beer

250g of anchovies

1 teaspoon ground mace

1 teaspoon ground cloves

2 teaspoons ground black pepper

2 teaspoons sea salt

30g fresh ginger (chopped)

200g shallots

500g fine mushrooms (roasted)

Method

Add everything to a large pan.

Bring to a rolling boil and continue until the quantity is reduced by half.

Put in a blender in small portions and blend until smooth-ish.

Transfer to wide-necked bottles.

Catsup or ketchup is a condiment based on just about anything...

Cherry Marmalade

Anon

At the time this recipe was written, the term 'marmalade' referred to any jam made with any fruit.

The extension of 'marmalade' in the English language to refer to citrus fruits was made in the 17th century when citrus first began to be plentiful enough in England for the usage to become common.

So here is a simple recipe for cherry jam.

Ingredients

1kg cherries (stoned)
1kg jam sugar

Method

Mix equal weights of cherries and jam sugar in a jam pan or other thick-bottomed pan.

Heat very gently, stirring all the time, until the juice from the cherries dissolves the sugar.

Then raise the heat and boil rapidly for about 5 mins whilst stirring, until the setting point is reached.

Remove any scum then put into warmed, clean jars.

Put on a waxed disc and seal.

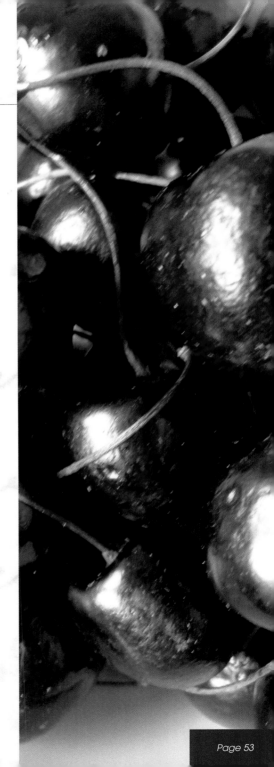

Curaçao

William Sayer

Curaçao is a liqueur flavoured with the dried peel of the laraha citrus fruit, grown on the island of Curaçao. A non-native plant similar to an orange, the laraha developed from the sweet Valencia orange transplanted by Spanish explorers. Although the bitter flesh of the laraha is all but inedible, the peels are aromatic and flavourful, maintaining much of the essence of the Valencia orange.

Curaçao liqueur was first developed and marketed by the Senior family in the 19th century.

To create the liqueur, the laraha peel is dried, bringing out the sweetly-fragranced oils. After soaking in a still with alcohol and water for several days, the peel is removed and other spices are added.

This recipe uses seville and sweet oranges to give flavour and is not as strong as the original since syrup is added.

The original recipe also called for three teaspoons of red barley, 'roasted for colour', but I omitted this as it is just for appearance and red barley is difficult to find. I have also halved the amounts in the original, but feel free to revert.

Although the bitter flesh of the laraha is all but inedible, the peels are aromatic and flavourful...

Ingredients

1 bottle of pale brandy

2 seville oranges

1 sweet orange

350g of sugar

2 inch stick of cinnamon

900mls water

Method

Place the oranges where they will dry very gradually until thoroughly dry when they will be 'not larger than a pigeon's egg.'

I put mine in the airing cupboard, but it takes some time. If you put them in a low oven, be careful that they do not burn. Then add them with the brandy and cinnamon to a large sealed jar and leave in a warm place for a week or two.

When you are ready to make the Curaçao, remove the oranges and strain the liquid through muslin to remove the cinnamon.

Make a very clear syrup of the sugar and water, but not strong enough to crystalise.

Cool, add the brandy then mix it all together and store it in a sealed bottle.

I'm not sure what to do with the used oranges. It seems a shame to throw them away, perhaps they would make good Christmas decorations? All suggestions welcome.

Currie Powder

William Sayer

This caught my eye so I had to make some up. I was also fascinated by the Grains of Paradise, which I had never heard of before.

Grains of Paradise - also known as alligator pepper, Guinea grains, or *melegueta peppe* - are peppery seeds from the leafy *Aframomum Melegueta* plant. They have been used in their native West Africa for centuries, and in Europe since at least the 800s. Today, they are commonly in use in Northern Africa but less abundant in Europe.

The name comes from Medieval spice traders looking for a way to inflate the price - it was claimed that these peppery seeds grew only in Eden, and had to be collected as they floated down the rivers out of paradise.

Although Grains of Paradise are now fairly rare and expensive, they used to be used as a cheaper substitute for black pepper. They have a zesty flavour, with hints of flowers, coriander and cardamom. You can use freshly ground pepper, sansho powder (prickly ash powder) or cardamom as a substitute.

William comments 'This is the best currie powder I ever used.' He could be right. It is a medium heat and is used just like any other curry powder.

As a marinade and paste for chicken I used 2 tablespoons mixed with 2 crushed cloves of garlic and lemon juice, and for a vegetable curry I used 1 tablespoon. The quantities here produce just over 400g.

Ingredients

260g Turmeric

10g Cayenne powder

6g Cloves

12g Cinnamon

10g Grains of Paradise

95g Coriander Seeds

6g Ground Ginger

10g Cummin Seed

6g Fennel Seed

Method

You can either use pre-ground or whole spices. Grind the whole seeds and spices then add the ready-ground spices.

Give them a short pulse with an electric grinder or pound carefully in a pestle. Can't you just smell it now?

Store in air-tight containers.

1900 – 1930

The Background

At the beginning of the century, Britain was coming out of the reign of Queen Victoria who had been on the throne for 63 years, and the first half of the 20th century was carved by war and unrest.

The First World War saw whole generations of young men disappear temporarily or permanently, changing the whole balance of the population, swiftly followed by the Influenza pandemic of 1918-19. The general strike in 1926 reflected the mood of the times.

At the start of the 20th century, malnutrition was widespread. Although the importance of clean water and good drainage were recognised, little was known about the dangers of a bad diet. During the First World War it was found that almost half the men called up to enlist were not in good enough health to serve.

It was also a time of great inventions – the radio, television and talking pictures.

The Kitchen

Until the development of the domestic refrigerator, fresh food was bought daily and the preservation of food proved a considerable problem. The first household refrigerator in the United Kingdom was sold in 1924, although at this time they were regarded as a luxury for most homes.

The early 20th century also saw the change from the kitchen range to the gas cooker, so recipes start to talk of cooking 'over a low heat' rather than 'over a low fire.'

By the end of this period, the British kitchen had changed dramatically, mainly due to the lack of household staff, changes in technology and the availability of foods.

Frozen foods were first marketed by Clarence Birdseye (who was previously a taxidermist) in the twenties.

Le Creuset was founded in France by Armand Desaegher (a casting specialist) and Octave Aubecq (an enameling specialist) in 1925, and is still popular today.

The Recipes

Again the recipes here had a preponderance of cakes, perhaps because these needed more careful note of the quantities of ingredients, whereas meat dishes rarely needed their methods to be noted.

Sweets, Cakes & Biscuits

Soups, Stews & Savouries

Puddings

Pickles & Preserves

Drinks

Extras

Meal Cakes

Mrs Berry

These cakes partly use wholemeal flour which was cheaper than the white flour to reduce the cost. They are bit like a cross between a scone and a rock cake.

Ingredients

200g plain flour
75g wholemeal flour
75g butter
1 teaspoon of baking powder
125g castor sugar
1 egg
50ml milk

Method

Preheat the oven to 190°C/375°F/Gas 5.

Mix all the dry ingredients together and rub in the butter until the mix is like breadcrumbs.

Add the egg and the milk and bring the dough together. Alternatively, put all the ingredients in a food processer and blitz until the mix comes together.

Roll out on a floured surface to around 1 cm thick and cut into small cakes.

Transfer to a lightly greased baking tray and bake for 25 minutes until lightly browned

These spread, so don't put them too close together.

Nice sliced in half with a bit of butter.

Spion Cops

Mrs Berry, but attributed to May Mills

These little cakes are very sweet and seem to be a version of coconut pyramids. Were they named after the battle of Spion Kop, fought during the Boer War?

The Battle of Spion Kop was fought about 24 miles west-south-west of Ladysmith on the hilltop of Spioenkop along the Tugela River, Natal in South Africa from 23–24 January 1900.

It was fought between the South African Republic and the Orange Free State on the one hand and British forces during the Second Boer War campaign to relieve Ladysmith, and resulted in a British defeat.

Makes you wonder why someone would name a cake after a defeat?

Ingredients:

250g coconut (desiccated)
250g castor sugar
2 lightly-beaten eggs

Method:

Preheat the oven to 190°C/375°F/Gas 5.

Easy to make and a good one for the children - just mix the ingredients together.

I made them into little hills by making moulds out of eggcups, but if you want a larger cake you could use a small coffee cup or other mould.

Put a sheet of rice or potato paper on a baking sheet and put the cakes about a centimetre apart (they spread a little.)

Cook for 15mins, when they will be golden on top. Leave them to cool on the tray before cutting them apart. If you are neat, you can cut round each cake.

A tasty treat, named for a Boer War defeat?

Mrs Smith's Ginger Nuts

Lucy Brown

A British staple, this recipe for Ginger Nuts caught my eye because it seems to be the same recipe my mother was using in the 1950s.

This is an easy peasy recipe and a good one to make with children.

Ingredients:

125g self-raising flour

50g margarine

25g sugar

2 tablespoon golden syrup

1 teaspoon ginger

1 teaspoon baking soda

Method:

Preheat the oven to 190°C/375°F/Gas 5.

Put the dry ingredients and margarine into a food processor and whizz until the mix is the consistency of breadcrumbs.

Add the golden syrup (if it is a cold day, warm it a little by putting the tin into some hot water) and continue mixing for a minute or so until the mix holds together.

Empty the mixture onto a floured surface. Bring together and roll out until it is about ½ cm thick.

Cut in rounds and place on a greased baking tray.

Bake in a moderate oven for 15-20 minutes until they are a dark golden brown.

The biscuits will be a little floppy when they come out of the oven; transfer them to a rack and they will crisp up as they cool.

An easy peasy recipe and a good one to make with children...

Spiced Treacle Scones

Lucy Brown

Scones or scones?

Whichever way you say it, these are absolutely delicious and having found this recipe, I have made it a lot!

Good old Lucy Brown, who notes that she got the recipe from 'a bulletin.' They are not as sweet as some scones, which I like.

Ingredients

250g plain flour,

30g margarine

30g sugar

1 rounded teaspoon each of baking soda and cream of tartar

1 level teaspoon each of ground ginger, cinnamon and mixed spice

1 rounded tablespoon treacle

80ml warm milk (you may need a little more if the mix is dry)

Method

Pre-heat the oven to 200°C/400°F/Gas 6.

Rub the margarine and flour together until they form a texture like soft breadcrumbs

Add the dry ingredients, mixing well.

Warm the treacle and mix it with the milk, then combine the lot, still mixing well, until you have a fairly stiff dough. Don't overwork it.

Turn onto a floured board, knead a small amount and roll out to about 1cm thickness, then cut out the scones using a cutter. Press straight down with the cutter, don't twist it, or the scones will come out lopsided.

Place on a greased baking tray in the middle of the oven for 15–20 minutes.

Self raising flour can be used, but then omit the cream of tartar and baking soda.

I asked the maid in dulcet tone
To order me a buttered scone,
The silly girl has been and gone
And ordered me a buttered scone...

Batchelor Cake

Lucy Brown

I don't know where the name came from, but this is a rich fruit cake. Although there were a lot of recipes for fruit cake among all the recipes I looked at, this seemed very straightforward. You will need a large bowl to make this cake.

Ingredients

500g flour

500g currants

125g mixed peel

250g butter (soft)

250g sultanas

250g sugar

4 eggs (beaten)

Rind of 1 lemon

1 teaspoon each cinnamon & mixed spice

1 dessertspoon treacle

1 teaspoon baking soda

100ml milk

Method

Preheat oven to 160°C / 325°F/ Gas 3.

Beat the butter & sugar to a pale cream. Add dry ingredients, eggs and milk.

Add the baking soda last. The mix should be quite stiff.

Spoon it into an 8' (20cm) round cake tin, preferably a springform, that has been greased.

Bake in the middle shelf for 3 hours or longer. Test the cake by poking it with a skewer to check when it is finally cooked - if the skewer comes out clean, the cake is ready.

Green Pea Soup

Anon

The smoothness of this depends on the sieving. if you're not too bothered, you can use a blender.

Ingredients

400g peas (fresh or frozen)

Few leaves of lettuce

A few leaves of spinach or chard

A small onion

A big sprig of mint

25g butter

1 litre vegetable stock

1 tablespoon cream

Method

Slice the onion and sauté with the spinach or chard, the mint and the lettuce (I used half a little gem), in butter.

When tender, add the peas and cook for 5 more minutes.

When cooked, pass through a sieve or blender.

Return to the pan and add the stock. Reheat, but don't boil.

Add a tablespoonful of cream, plus pepper and salt to taste.

Serve very hot.

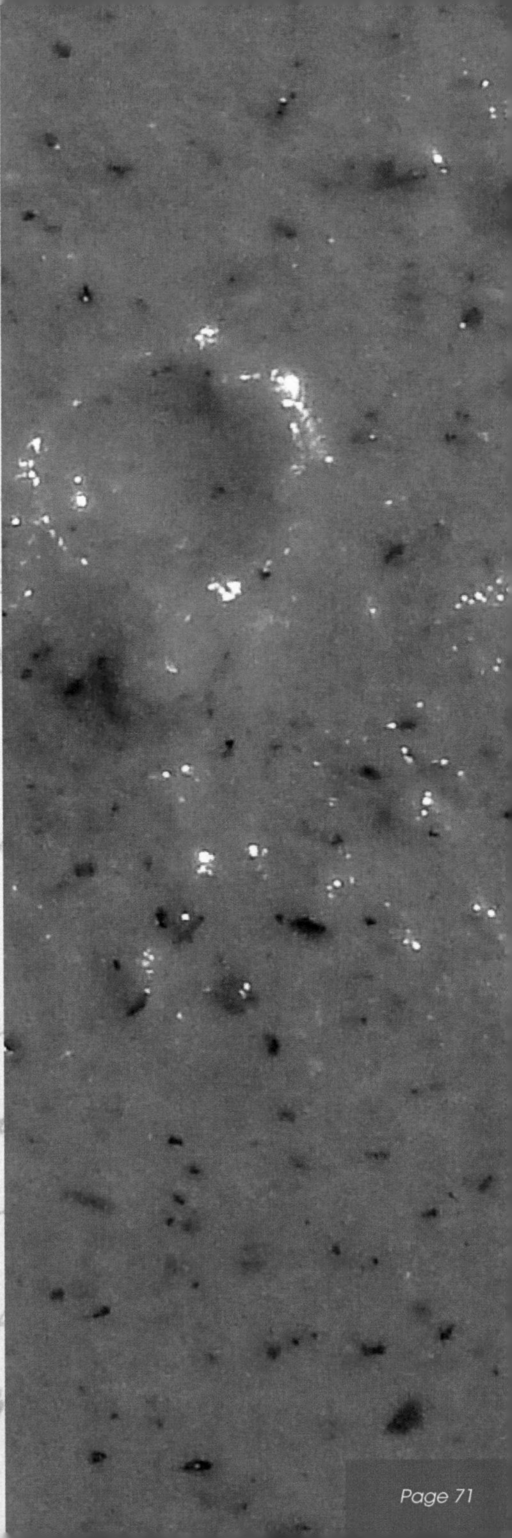

Giblet Soup

Anon

Now don't turn your nose up before you have tasted this!

Forget the turkey at Christmas and just have the soup?

Ingredients

Giblets from chicken or turkey or duck

100g bacon or lardons

1 onion (stuck with 3 cloves)

2 pieces mace

Sprig of thyme

Sprig of parsley or parsley stalks

1 large bay leaf

A stick of celery

6 black peppercorns

1.5 litres good chicken stock

A wine glass of sherry (no, not the 250ml glass...)

Salt and pepper

Method

Fry the giblets with the bacon in a large pan, until browned.

Add the onion, spices and herbs.

Add the stock, put on the lid and simmer for around 45 minutes.

Strain and return to the pan. Taste and season. Leave the salt until the very end, as the stock and bacon will probably provide all the salt that you need.

Add the sherry a few minutes before you serve and allow to warm through.

Now don't turn your nose up before you have tasted this....

Potted Meat Paste

Mrs Berry

The process in the original recipe for this paste was laborious - cooking the meat in a jar in water for a day, mincing the cooked meat then pounding it in a mortar - but with modern equipment it's very easy to make.

A good addition to *hors d'oeuvres,* or tasty as a starter with toast, it's a real example of how modern kitchen equipment can make our lives easier.

Ingredients

1kg steak (shoulder steak lean)

3 dessertspoons cold water

Salt & pepper

4g mace

1 bay leaf (optional)

Butter for sealing the jars

Method

Put all the ingredient into a slow cooker on low setting for around 8 hours.

Remove the bay leaf (if used) and transfer the meat to a food processor.

Blend well, adding the gravy until it is the texture you want. Season well too - don't be a salt miser with this.

Put in clean pots and cover with melted butter. Store in the fridge, where it will keep for a couple of weeks, or freeze. If you are freezing, put in plastic containers, not glass.

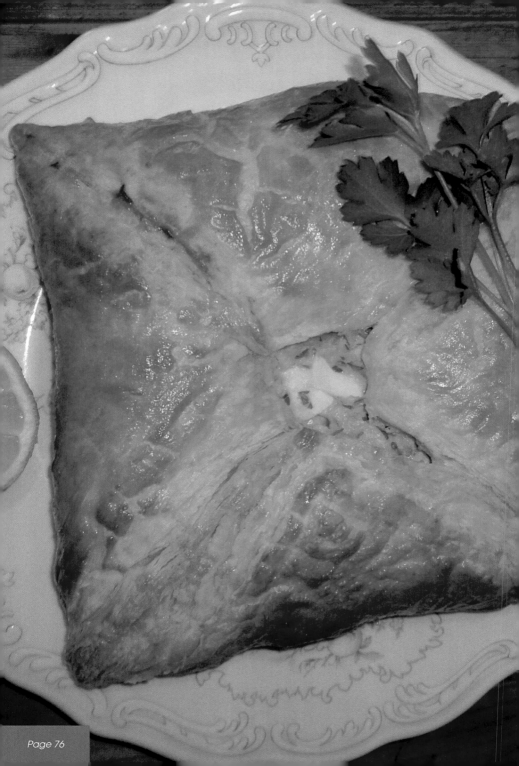

Fish Pastry

Mrs Berry

This recipe had a note that it was learned 'at a gas lecture.' When gas oven manufacturers were trying to encourage housewives to turn to gas for cooking (which was seen as dangerous), they had representatives giving talks and demonstrations around the country to boost sales. The period between 1900 and 1930 saw the biggest take-up of gas cookers, by which time electric cookers were coming onto the market.

Ingredients

500g rough puff pastry
250g fish, raw or cooked
2 hard-boiled eggs
A tablespoon of chopped parsley
Squeeze of lemon juice
Salt & pepper
100ml white sauce, cold
Egg wash for colouring

Method

Pre-heat the oven to 190°C/375°F/Gas 5.

Flake the fish and chop the eggs.

In a bowl, roughly mix together the fish, chopped eggs, white sauce and parsley.

Season to taste with salt and pepper, then add a squeeze of lemon juice.

Roll the pastry into a large square, large enough that it will take the fish mixture and have enough left to wrap it like a parcel.

Place the pastry on a well-oiled baking sheet. Put mixture in the middle, wet round the edges of the pastry then bring corners to the middle and seal well along the seams - but leave a small hole in the top.

Paint with egg wash to give a shiny golden crust when cooked.

Bake for 35–40 minutes until golden.

Salmon does very well for this recipe, as does smoked haddock and pollock.

This recipe has a note that it was learned 'at a gas lecture.'

Kidney à la Villars

Anon

This can be eaten for breakfast for four or as a main meal for two. The tomato sauce recipe included corralin and carmine for colour which I have left out. Who said food was more natural in the past?

Ingredients

4 lambs' kidneys

4 slices smoked back bacon

1 beaten egg

Flour & breadcrumbs for coating

Salt & pepper to season

Vegetable oil for frying

For the tomato sauce:

2 or 3 tomatoes (peeled and deseeded)

25g butter

Salt & pepper

1 dessertspoon of tarragon vinegar

300ml lamb stock or gravy

1 finely chopped shallot

1 teaspoon cornflour

Method:

Remove the skin and cores of the kidneys. If large, cut each one into three slices lengthways - otherwise just cut in half.

Season well with salt and pepper, dip into the flour, then in the beaten eggs and sprinkle with freshly-made breadcrumbs.

Grill the bacon.

Put the vegetable oil in a frying pan and bring to a medium heat. Fry the kidneys to a golden brown - about 3 minutes on each side - then serve with rice layered with the bacon and cover with the tomato sauce.

To make the tomato sauce:

Put the tomatoes in a saucepan with the butter, a little salt, the tarragon vinegar, the stock and the chopped shallot.

Simmer until the tomatoes are cooked, then pass this through a tammy or sieve. Return the sauce to the saucepan to get thoroughly hot.

Mix the cornflour with a little water and add a little at a time until the sauce is the thickness you like. Add salt and pepper to taste.

Kromskies

Anon

From the word Russian *kromochka*, diminutive of *kroma* - slice of bread. The recipe says 'Kromskies are croquettes cooked in the Russian manner.' Normally croquettes are dipped in egg and breadcrumbs, but these are wrapped in ham and fried in batter. Pretty high in calories, but tasty.

I made them about the size of a sausage but you can make mini ones for snacks or bigger for a main meal. The size is up to you and might depend on the size of the slices of ham.

Ingredients

200g any cold meat, fish or poultry

Thinly-cut ham

Batter

Salt & pepper to taste

Oil for frying

For the batter:

125g plain flour

150ml milk

25g butter

pinch of salt

1 egg

Method

For the batter:

Place the flour and salt in a basin.

In another basin, beat the egg, add the milk, then pour onto the flour, stirring well all the time.

Lastly add the butter.

For the filling:

Mince the remains of any cold meat, fish or poultry, season with pepper & salt and shape like a sausage.

Take some slices of cold ham - as thin as possible - and wrap the croquettes. A good tip here is to stab each one with a bamboo skewer, cocktail stick or similar to stop them springing apart during cooking.

Dip each one in the frying batter. Fry until golden, then when crisp and brown, arrange on a hot dish and serve immediately.

Kedgeree: A Breakfast Dish

Anon

No Edwardian costume drama would be complete without the breakfast sideboard scene.

This classic breakfast dish was of course brought back from India, that far flung post of the Empire. There have been lots of versions of this dish but I wanted to include it as just so typical of the times.

I was taken with the types of fish recommended - this doesn't come from a poor home. I know I don't have much left-over turbot at a weekend.

This is quite a simple version - after all it was a breakfast dish - so you can tart it up as you wish.

Ingredients

1 cup of basmati rice
4 hard boiled eggs
100-200g any cold cooked fish
25g butter
Pepper and salt

Method

Boil a cupful of rice until tender.

Boil four eggs until hard, cool and peel them and when cold chop them into small pieces.

Take the remains of any cold fish, flake it and mix together with the rice and eggs.

Put the mixture in a pan, with a knob of butter, heat it until thoroughly cooked, stirring it constantly to prevent it burning.

Season well with pepper and salt and serve it quickly while hot. Take care not to make it too moist.

No Edwardian costume drama would be complete without the breakfast sideboard scene.

Blackberries Pudding

Mrs Berry

I have reduced the salt in the pastry for our modern tastes. This is absolutely delicious with either custard or cream.

For the pastry:

175g plain flour

30g margarine

½ teaspoon salt

¾ teaspoon baking powder

4 tablespoons water

For the filling;

500g blackberries (or as many as you can cram in)

50g sugar

3 tablespoons of water

Method:

Make the pastry. Put all of the dry ingredients into a bowl and rub together until it looks like breadcrumbs. Add the water and mix together either with a knife or with your hands. Don't overwork.

Divide into ⅔ and ⅓. Roll the larger piece out to a circle until about ½ centimetre thick.

Grease a basin well and line with the pastry. Add the blackberries, sugar and water. Roll out the remaining piece of pastry to form a lid and put on the dish. Pinch the edges of the pastry together.

If the basin you have used has a lid, just cover over with greased paper and put on the lid. If it hasn't then cover over with greased paper and tie on a rag. Put the basin in a pan and steam (with water 3 parts up the basin) for 1½ hours.

Puddings are especially cheap when you can use berries from the hedgerow.

Coffee Cream

Anon

This delicious desert is the consistency of panna cotta but lighter, using milk and cream. The recipe called for strong coffee so I use instant for ease

Instant, or soluble coffee was invented and patented in 1890 by David Strang of New Zealand, so it would have been available for the cook to use. Mind you, early versions did not dissolve very easily and would have needed straining and real instant coffee wasn't introduced to England until the 1930s.

Ingredients

300ml milk

2 egg yolks

4 leaves of gelatine

75g sugar

150ml strong coffee made with 3 teaspoons of instant coffee

300ml whipping cream

Method

Mix together the egg yolks and the sugar. Add to the milk and heat in a pan, stirring constantly until it thickens and coats the back of the spoon. Do not boil, as it might split.

Soak the gelatine leaves in cold water and when soggy, squeeze out the excess water and add to the hot coffee. Add this to the custard and cool.

Whip the cream until it is thick but not stiff and stir lightly into the custard.

Pour into a wet mould or individual moulds and pop in the fridge to set. If you want it to be stiffer, just use an extra gelatine leaf.

Now try not to eat it all at once!

Tip: If your custard does split...

...turn it into a fresh bowl and put the bowl in a sink filled with ice cubes and cold water (sink, not bowl - oh, you know what I mean.) Whisk with a balloon whisk and all will be well. If not, then a spoonful of cornflour added to some cream whisked in whilst rewarming very gently might do the trick.

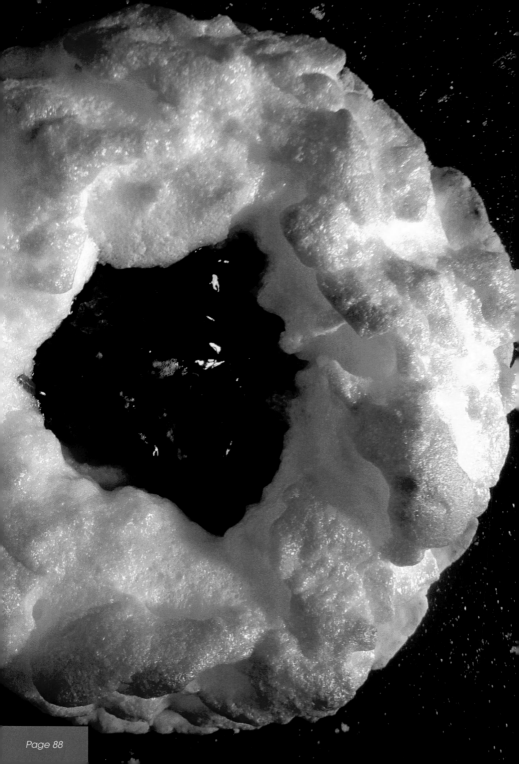

Felixstowe Tart

Mrs Berry

This recipe called for ½ teaspoon of Paisley flour made by Brown & Polson of Paisley. It is a version of baking powder, although there are no details of the mixture. I have used self raising flour. This is an easy little tart to make.

Ingredients

75g butter

75g Self raising flour

75g cornflour

20g caster sugar

2 eggs

Jam

Method

Preheat the oven to 220°C/425°F/Gas 7.

Mix the flour, cornflour, butter and half the sugar together with a fork, then add the egg yolks and mix to a soft dough.

Roll out on a floured board to the size of a tea plate.

Transfer to a greased baking sheet. Pinch the edges with your finger and thumb to make a little ridge round the edge and prick all over with a fork.

Bake until golden, about 10 – 15 minutes.

Then put a dollop of jam in the middle - how much and what kind is up to your preferences.

Whisk the egg whites, add the remaining sugar and continue whisking until it is stiff to make the miringue.Pile it around the jam.

Return the tart to the oven until the meringue is browned, about 5–10 minutes.

Mock Mango Chutney

Mrs Berry

This is a lovely sweet, fruity chutney. As mangoes were exhorbitantly expensive for the normal household, plums gave a fruity chutney to be used where mango chutney normally would be - for example with the curries that had been brought back from the Empire.

Ingredients

500g cooking plums

125g dates

10g salt

250g brown sugar

1 medium onion

¼ teaspoon pepper

½ teaspoon ground ginger

150ml vinegar - Any vinegar will be fine, I used half white wine vinegar and black mulberry vinegar which gave it even more of a fruity flavour.

Method

Halve the plums and remove the stones. Cook gently in the vinegar, then strain.

Chop the dates and the onion and cook in the same vinegar then add salt and sugar

Replace the plums and add the ginger and pepper. Mix together well.

Replace over the heat, bring to the boil and then simmer until mixture is well blended and thickens. Bottle and seal while hot.

The colour of this chutney depends on the colour of the plums.

Blackberry Vinegar

Anon

Blackberries in season were made the most of, and this cook was no exception. I liked this one.

Ingredients

Blackberries

Vinegar (enough to cover the fruit)

Sugar (450g of sugar for every 600ml of juice after steeping)

Method

Pick fruit in fine weather and steep for five days in sufficient vinegar to cover. I used white wine vinegar but you can use red wine vinegar or cider vinegar.

Strain through muslin and add the sugar.

Bring gently to the boil to dissolve the sugar and allow to simmer for five minutes. Pour into sterilised bottles.

Ginger Beer

Anon

Ginger beer recipes abound in these hand-written books. This sounded like a good one.

Ingredients

250g root ginger

125g cream of tartar

4 lemons

1.5kg sugar

25g yeast

10 litres of boiling water

Method

Peel the lemons thinly and bruise the ginger.

Cover with water and boil for 10 minutes, then put into a bucket with the sugar, cream of tartar, lemon juice and the boiling water.

When cool, add the yeast by floating a thick piece of towel with the yeast on top. Leave for twelve hours, then stir.

Filter into bottles and seal - the ginger beer will be ready in two days.

Salad Cream

Anon

This is the real English salad cream.

It is a particularly British taste as a salad dressing and a sandwich spread, and was only introduced to the USA in 2000 when expats called for it.

Heinz Salad Cream was the first commercial brand developed exclusively for the UK market in 1914, so this year celebrates its 100th birthday.

Due to the higher cost of ingredients during periods of rationing in the United Kingdom, a flavour similar to mayonnaise was achieved by the creation of salad cream. Rules were made about the amount of oil and eggs that had to be included in the mix in order to call a product salad cream.

I like the way the recipes asks for olive oil 'where obtainable.' I have reduced the sugar to suit modern tastes.

I like the way the recipe asks for olive oil 'where obtainable'

Ingredients

2 tablespoons sugar

2 teaspoons mustard

½ teaspoon ground black pepper

½ teaspoon salt

2 heaped teaspoons corn flour

2 egg yolks

1 cup of water

1 cup of white wine vinegar

2 tablespoons olive oil

150ml cream

Method

Mix all the dry ingredients, then add the egg yolks.

Put into a food processor and add water and vinegar gradually to make a smooth mix, then add the olive oil.

Pour into a pan and bring to the boil over a medium heat, stirring constantly until it forms a thick sauce.

Cool, stir in the cream, then transfer to a sealable bottle with a wide neck.

Despite the addition of cream, It will keep in the fridge for up to six months.

1930 – 1950

The Background

The watchword here is austerity.

Following the first World War, a lack of workforce and the depression meant that times were lean for most kitchens. Big houses could no longer afford pre-war staffing numbers, and unemployment was high, hitting 2 million. The Jarrow march to London took place in protest.

During the war, bringing women into the workplace meant they had less time to cook. Less time, combined with less choice of ingredients because of rationing during the second World War meant that cooks had to become more canny and inventive with what they had. Fuel was also rationed.

The Kitchen

The 1930s saw the mass-production of electric kitchen appliances. By 1939, a quarter of all kitchens had a refrigerator. Labour-saving devices were popular, including mincing machines, potato-peelers, apple-corers and knife-sharpeners.

New foods included self-raising flour, dried yeast, baking powder, jelly, custard powder, lentils, pickles, margarine and dried vegetables. Breakfast cereals became popular, and the Shredded Wheat Company opened a factory in Welwyn Garden City.

Instant coffee was first sold in England in 1939, leading to a dramatic rise in its popularity, and sliced bread was first sold.

For most of this period, foods were rationed and this obviously had a great impact on what and how foods were cooked.

The Recipes

Sweets, Cakes & Biscuits

Soups, Stews & Savouries

Puddings

Pickles & Preserves

Extras

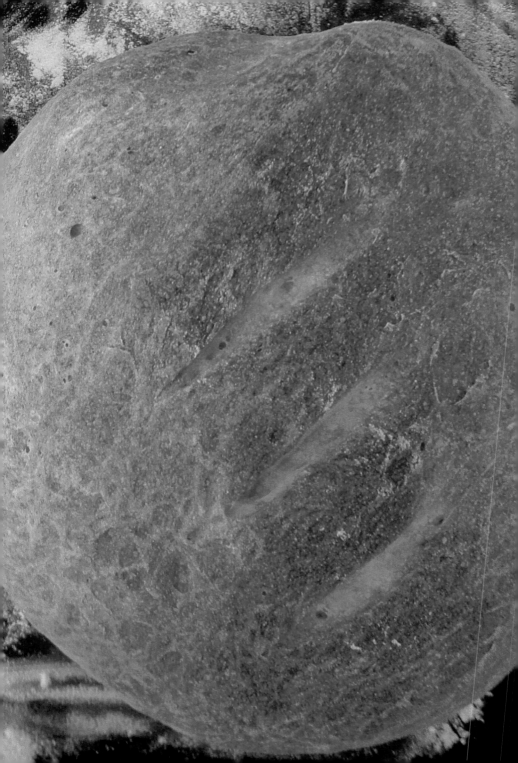

Potato Bread

Anon

As potatoes weren't on ration until later in the war they were used to eke out other recipes. This produces a delicious, light, crispy loaf that is worth making anyway. Crispy and tasty.

Ingredients

500g strong bread flour

250g potatoes

1 x sachet dried yeast

100ml water

1½ teaspoons salt

Method

Boil the potatoes, then pass them through a sieve or mash them very well.

Mix the potatoes with the flour, yeast and salt while they are still hot.

Add the water and bring together into a dough.

Knead the dough for around 10 minutes, until it is smooth and elastic.

Put in a bowl, cover and allow to rise for around an hour or until doubled in size.

Knock out the air, cut in half and knead each half for a few more minutes to form two loaves.

Put the loaves on a floured baking sheet and leave to rise for another hour or so, until doubled in size again.

Score the tops with a sharp knife and the loaves are ready for the oven.

Bake for 30 minutes at 220°C/425°F/Gas 7.

The bread is ready when its is browned and sounds hollow when tapped on the bottom.

Barley Scones

Anon

Barley meal is a wholemeal barley flour lighter than wheat meal but darker in colour. Interestingly, the word *barn*, originally meant 'barley-house.'

Barley was used as an early form of measurement.
Five poppy seeds made a barleycorn and three or four barleycorns made an inch.

These scones do not rise as well as wheat flour scones, but have a nice nutty flavour. Just don't expect tall scones.

This recipe can also be made using ¾ barley flour to ¼ white plain flour.

Ingredients

250g barley flour
250g white flour
80g butter
40g sugar
2 x teaspoons baking powder
Pinch of salt
150ml milk

Method

Preheat the oven to 220°C/425°F/Gas 7.

Rub the butter and flour together, add the sugar, salt and baking powder and mix through.

Add the milk to make a stiff dough.

Roll out to about 1cm thick and cut into rounds using a cutter. The trick here is not to twist the cutter but to tap it down sharply. Twisting it will make the scones lopsided as they cook.

Place on a greased baking tray and bake for 12–15 minutes

Transfer to a wire rack to cool.

Five poppy seeds made a barleycorn and three or four barleycorns made an inch.

Bishop's Bread

Kochrecepts

Bishop's bread and Bishop's wine are traditional holiday treats associated with the feast of St. Nicholas. Both delicacies arose in Germany and parts of Eastern Europe.

Bishop's bread is a sweetened bread, often containing raisins and/or currants. Although any bought or homemade cake decorated with the Bishop's name and a tiny mitre can be used on the feast of a Bishop-saint, the traditional cake is *Bischofsbrot* or 'Bishop's Bread.'

This recipe asks you to 'beat the sugar with the eggs for ½ hour!' Thanks heavens for electric mixers.

Ingredients

140g sugar

4 eggs

140g sultanas

140g blanched almonds cut in strips

60g candied peel

140g plain flour

1 teaspoon baking powder

Method

Preheat the oven to 180°C/350°F/Gas 4.

Beat the sugar with the eggs until pale and creamy.

Toss the sultanas and almonds in a little of the flour.

Fold the flour into the egg and sugar mix, then add the sultanas, almonds and candied peel and stir in lightly.

Pour into a well-buttered 8inch/20cm springform tin and bake for 50 minutes.

Test after 45 minutes and cover with foil if the top is browning too much.

Gingerbread

Kochrecepts

As this recipe was from the German recipe notebook, the home of gingerbread, I just had to include it. It is a light cake made with golden syrup rather than treacle.

Ingredients

250g plain flour

250g golden syrup

60g butter

15g caster sugar

½ teaspoon ground ginger

½ teaspoon ground mixed spice

½ teaspoon bicarbonate of soda

150ml milk

Method

Preheat the oven to 175°C/350°F/Gas 4.

Grease a square tin, 25cm/9 inches.

The mix needs to go straight in the oven after mixing, so everything needs to be ready.

Warm the milk and golden syrup gently in a small pan. This just needs to be warm to the touch, not hot - enough to melt the syrup in the milk.

Rub the fat into the flour, then add the spices and sugar. Combine with the milk and syrup mixture.

Add the soda and mix as quickly as possible.

Transfer to the tin, put into the oven at once and bake for around 40 minutes.

Cut into squares in the tin, then remove and cool on a rack.

Winter Cake

Anon

In the northern hemisphere, hens will not lay many eggs in the winter unless artificial light is provided, as the number of light hours is greatly decreased.

So this eggless cake would have been a boon for those who kept chickens - and for those without chickens - when rationing came in.

Ingredients

250g flour

125g sultanas

50g sugar

50g butter

1 teaspoon bicarbonate of soda

1 dessertspoon vinegar

200ml milk

Method

Preheat the oven to 180°C/350°F/Gas 4.

This is very easy to make.

Beat the butter and sugar to a cream, then add the flour, the sultanas and the bicarbonate of soda by degrees. You should eventually have a mix with the texture of white breadcrumbs.

Sprinkle the vinegar over the mixture and add enough milk to mix well to a soft dropping consistency.

Beat thoroughly, and transfer to a 1lb loaf tin.

Bake for one hour and test with a skewer before removing from the oven.

As an alternative finish, sprinkle Demerara sugar on the surface before cooking.

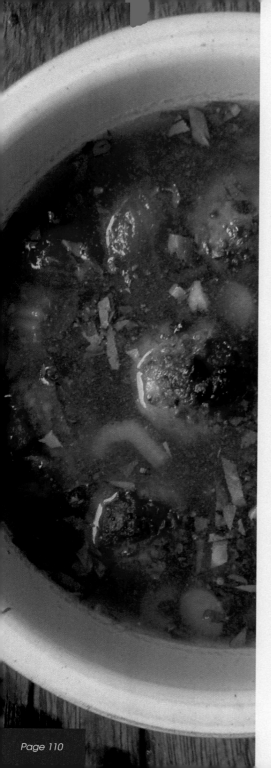

Spanish albondigas soup is actually a traditional Mexican meatball soup ('albondigas' means 'meatballs' in Spanish.) It is a Mexican version of comfort food.

What makes the flavour of albondigas soup distinctive is the chopped mint in the meatballs. You can, of course, skip the mint, substitute with a little fresh oregano or some coriander. You can also vary the vegetables added, depending on what you have on hand and what's in season.

This recipe also includes eggballs. Never seen that before.

As always, this is one of those recipes where everyone has their own favourite version so feel free to customise it. Don't scrimp on the stock though - use a good one.

Meatballs

500g minced beef

1 medium onion (finely chopped)

A good grating of nutmeg

½ tablespoon fresh chopped mint

½ tablespoon fresh chopped parsley

Good seasoning of salt and pepper

1 egg

Spanish Albondigas Soup

G Watson

Eggballs

Lemon

4 eggs

Salt & pepper to taste

Soup

2 litres stock (chicken or vegetable)

2 stalks celery

2 carrots

3 tomatoes, peeled and deseeded

1 tablespoon fresh chopped oregano

1 tablespoon roughly chopped parsley

½ teaspoon ground black pepper

A blade of mace

Salt & pepper to taste

Method

Meatballs - Mix all the ingredients well in a bowl. To make sure you have the right seasoning, take a little bit and fry it as a taster, then adjust the seasoning accordingly before you go on. Make the mix into golfball size balls.

Eggballs – Hard boil 3 eggs and remove the yolks. Mix these with the raw yolk of the fourth egg, a few drops of lemon juice, salt and pepper. Make them into small balls the size of a walnut.

Put them into simmering water for around 2–3 minutes to harden.

Soup – Chop the celery and carrots into 1cm cubes. Add the stock to a large pan, then add the vegetables and cook for 5 minutes. Then add the oregano and half the parsley, the spices and season.

Add the meatballs and keep the soup at a simmer for around 10 minutes (15 minutes if you have kept the meatballs in the fridge.)

Test one of the meatballs to make sure they are cooked through.

Add the eggballs (carefully) and the remainder of the parsley and cook for another 5 minutes.

This recipe includes eggballs. Never seen that before...

Tomato Soup

Anon

This should actually be called tomato and bacon soup. Sorry vegetarians, but this is not a soup that would be improved by removing the bacon. In times of rationing, a good way to make a little bacon go a long way.

Ingredients

1kg tomatoes (peeled)

25g butter

25g bacon

1 carrot

1 onion

1 stick celery

1 litre of vegetable stock

Method

Melt the butter, cut the bacon and vegetables in slices and very slightly fry.

Add the stock and bring to the boil. Don't scrimp on the stock, always use a good one for soup.

Add pepper at this point but not salt - both the stock and the bacon are a little salty. Taste at the end and then only add salt if it needs it.

Simmer gently for 30 minutes.

Put in a blender until well blended. If you want your soup very smooth, follow that by putting through a sieve. I am not one to do unnecessary work but rubbing through a sieve actually does improve this soup and will take about 10 minutes.

Return to the pan, bring back to heat, taste and season.

Cheese Pudding

Anon

This is a sort of easy, day-to-day version of a cheese soufflé. It takes about 10 minutes to prepare, and you can use up leftover cheese and yesterday's bread. It goes nicely with either salad or green vegetables - why not try with Salad Fifii (page 156)?

Ingredients
125g grated cheese
35g breadcrumbs
300ml milk
2 medium eggs
½ teaspoon mustard powder
Salt and pepper

Method
Preheat the oven to 190°C/375°F/Gas 5.

Beat the eggs, and add them to the cheese, breadcrumbs, and mustard. Season to taste.

Boil the milk and add it to the rest of the ingredients, pour into a buttered baking dish and bake for about 30 minutes until puffed up and golden brown.

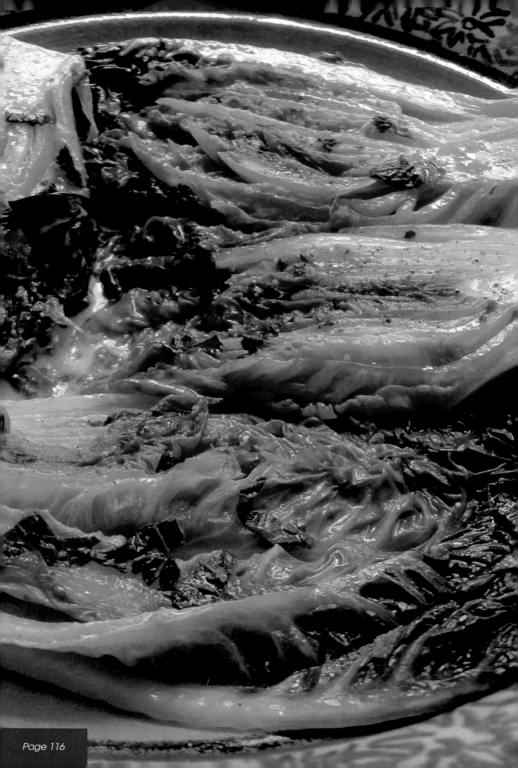

Casserole of Lettuce
Anon

The original recipe included the instruction 'cook gently until the lettuce is cooked – about an hour!' Still, we Brits do have a reputation for cooking green veg until it dissolves.

When cooked until the lettuce still has a bite, this is a tasty dish. The trick is definitely not to overcook the lettuce.

The original also suggests that a teaspoon of condensed milk may be added before serving - I suggest you don't!

Ingredients

2 large baby gem lettuces

50g butter

150ml milk

Salt and pepper

A pinch of nutmeg

1 teaspoonful of chopped mint

1 teaspoonful of cornflour (optional)

The original recipe included the instruction 'cook gently until the lettuce is cooked – about an hour'!

Method

Preheat the oven to 160°C/325°F/Gas 3.

Wash the lettuces, drain, and cut in half lengthways.

Blanche them in a saucepan of boiling salted water to which a pinch of salt has been added, then strain.

Put them into an ovenproof shallow dish with the butter and milk. Season, add the nutmeg and chopped mint.

Cover and cook very gently, in the oven for about 15-20 minutes until the lettuce is tender but still has bite to the heart, and serve in the casserole.

This can be served as it is or with the liquid made into a sauce.

To do this, pour off the milk into a small pan, add a teaspoon of cornflour, then pour over the lettuce.

I have also tried the recipe using vegetable stock and it is good.

Egg Pie

Anon

Like a lot of recipes in this section, Egg Pie was born out of a necessity brought about by rationing but actually reflects British comfort food. It just shows what you can make out of the store cupboard and with an inspired veg dish this will fill the family.

Method

4 hard boiled eggs

500g potatoes

4 onions, sliced

150ml white sauce

Salt and pepper

A small bunch of parsley

Method

Hard boil four eggs. Throw into cold water and remove the shells. Fry the onion slices until golden.

Boil and mash the potatoes with a little butter, minced parsley and season to taste. Spread a layer of this at the bottom of a pie dish, then put a lay er of the cooked onions spread on the potato.

Then put a layer of sliced eggs a little white sauce and more potato and repeat until the dish is full. Finish with potato on the top

Put a few bits of butter on the top & bake until really hot and brown.

Like a lot of recipes in this section, Egg Pie was born out of a necessity brought about by rationing...

Irish Potato Pudding

Anon

When meat was scarce, potatoes and cheese were a major part of a diet designed to fill on a short budget and rationing.

Ingredients

6 fair sized potatoes (or about 600g)

300ml hot milk

35g butter

50g grated cheese

2 eggs

Method

Cook the potatoes and pass through a sieve or mash very well until smooth.

Heat the milk with the butter until the butter has melted. Add this to the potato. The consistency will vary depending on the type of potato used, but it needs to be more liquid than normal mashed potato because the baking will make it stiffer.

Separate the eggs and whisk the whites until stiff.

When the potato is cool, mix in the grated cheese and the yolks of the eggs. The whites are then folded in and the whole placed in a deep dish.

Add a little grated cheese to the top and bake for 30-40 minutes at 190°C/375°F/Gas 5 until the top is golden brown.

Indian Trifle

Anon

There is no explanation as to why this is called Indian Trifle. Many dishes were ascribed to India or China which had 'exotic' ingredients such as banana. By the way, India is the world's largest producer of bananas.

The recipe called for six bananas but I think they must have been smaller then, as two did the job with the dish I used.

This is real nursery food. Bananas and custard always go down well.

Ingredients

1 tablespoon of ground rice

300ml milk

1 dessertspoon sugar

A small squeeze of lemon juice

Yolk of 1 egg

2 or 3 bananas

600mls custard

½ teaspoon vanilla extract

Method

Save a small amount of the milk and mix it with the egg yolk.

Boil 1 tablespoon of ground rice in half a pint of milk. Stir well so that there are no lumps.

Add sugar to sweeten, a few drops of lemon juice and the egg/milk mix.

When the rice is cooled a little after thoroughly cooking, put it in a glass dish.

Slice two or three bananas over the top. Over them, pour quite thick custard, sweetened and flavoured with a little vanilla Leave till cold.

If you can't get ground rice, just put some in the coffee grinder and grind it well.

Patriotic Pudding

Anon

This is the best sponge pudding recipe I have come across, light and tasty. I found a few recipes called Patriotic Pudding, each reflecting their times. This plain sponge pudding reflects the austerity of the times, whereas the Victorian version is a rich, fruit suet pudding.

Ingredients

1 egg
175g flour
125g butter
75g castor sugar
1 teaspoonful of baking powder
Two tablespoons of milk
2 tablespoons jam

Method

Cream the sugar and butter. Add flour and the egg (well beaten) by degrees, then the milk. Lastly, add the baking powder.

Grease a basin well and put two tablespoonsful of jam at the bottom. Pour the mixture over it.

Allow a 2 pint basin for this as the sponge doubles in size.

Steam for 1½ hours.

Mysterious Pudding

Kochrecepts

There is nothing really mysterious about this pudding. It is a sponge pudding with marmalade - a very good sponge pudding, mind. However, because it used the egg ration, it needed to be talked up.

As sponge puddings were filling and easy to make, they featured large in the diet of the time.

Ingredients

2 eggs

The weight of the eggs in plain flour, butter and castor sugar

1 teaspoonful baking powder

A good tablespoonful marmalade (or two if you really like marmalade)

Method

Separate the eggs.

In a mixing bowl, add the baking powder to the flour, then add the sugar and marmalade, the well beaten yolks and finally the stiffly-whipped whites of the eggs.

Butter a basin well, pour in the mix then cover the basin. If the basin doesn't have a lid,

cut a round of greaseproof paper two inches larger than the bowl, make a fold in the middle, cover the basin with it and tie it round the top.

Steam for 1½ hours in a pan with boiling water at about a third of the height of the basin. Turn out and spread with a little warmed, slightly watered-down marmalade.

Serve with custard. Never cream or ice cream, just custard.

WARTIME
CHUTNEY

Wartime Chutney

G Watson

Wartime meant doing what you could with what you had. The vegetables in this recipe were cheap and not rationed and to get tasty chutney to tart up boring food, it was worth using some of the precious sugar ration.

The Ministry of Food educated people with leaflets, radio programmes and community demonstrations on the latest and greatest food preserving techniques, to ensure that no food went to waste. Many people started saving up their sugar rations right at the start of the summer to help with preserving time. Some years, during the summer, the Ministry of Food was able to double the sugar rations to encourage home preserving.

Ingredients

750g swede, turnip, carrot and marrow

200g onion (chopped)

250g sugar

125g sultanas, figs or dates (chopped)

1 heaped tablespoon English mustard powder

1 heaped tablespoon ground ginger

600ml malt vinegar

Method

Grate half the vegetables and chop the rest into ½ cm cubes (ish – it's more important that the pieces are the same size than the actual size).

Remove the seeds from the marrow. Add the vegetables, onion, fruit and spices to a pan with the vinegar.

Boil until the vegetables are tender then add the sugar.

This is a hot spicy chutney so if you want something a little milder, reduce the mustard.

Blackberry Jelly

Anon

The apple water here provides the pectin to help the jelly set. This produces quite a soft jelly, but delicious.

Ingrdients

1 kg blackberries

500ml apple water (see below) to each litre of juice

1lb sugar to each pint of liquid

Method

The apple water is made by putting the peelings and cores of some apples (approx a kg) into a pan with 2–3 cloves and an inch-long stick of cinnamon. Cover with water and simmer until the apples are soft and the water has reduced by half, then strain.

Pick over the blackberries and remove any that are damaged. Put them into a pan with a thick bottom and simmer until the juice flows freely. Sstrain through a clean cloth for at least two hours, but preferably overnight.

Measure, and add 500ml of apple water to each litre of juice.

Bring to the boil gently to dissolve the sugar, then bring to a rolling boil. Cook, keeping well skimmed and removing any scum.

After 15 minutes, test for setting using a saucer that has been chilled in the fridge. Put a small blob on the saucer and leave to cool slightly. Gently push your fingertips through it - the surface will wrinkle if the jam is at setting point.

Remove the pan from the heat while testing - if the jelly overboils, it will become syrupy and will never set.

Go on testing every few minutes so that you don't overcook it. Jellies are better slightly loose than too thick.

Bottle in clean warmed jars and label.

Betty's Chocolate Spread

G Watson

I had to add this homemade chocolate spread, although it is perhaps too nice for my waistline. I did add more cocoa to make it chocolatier (is that a real word?) Easy to make and scrummy.

Ingredients

1 tablespoon soft butter

1 tablespoon icing sugar

2 tablespoons dried milk

2 teaspoons cocoa powder

1 tablespoon boiling water

Method

If the dried milk you are using is the granulated rather than fine powdered type, give it a whizz in the coffee grinder or smash it in a mortar. This makes it easier to mix in.

Put all of the dry ingredients in a bowl then add the boiling water and mix well, mashing it with the back of the spoon. It never is quite as smooth as the bought variety, but that doesn't affect the spreadability or taste.

Put it in a jar or small covered dish and keep in the fridge.

I don't know how long it lasts as it hasn't got past a week in my house.

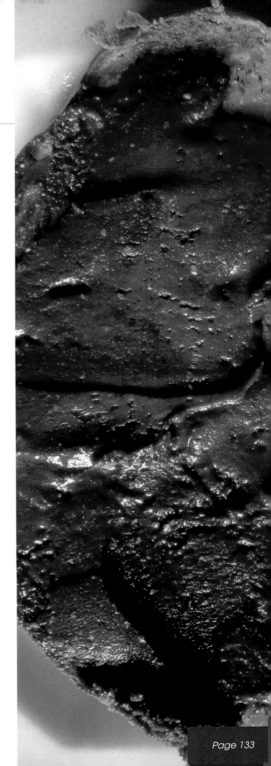

Elderberry Ketchup (Or Shrub)

G Watson

Although this is called ketchup, it's not like the sauce we know and love, but a spicy vinegar. Remove the shallots and it is a lovely drink called shrub - two recipes in one!

Vinegar as a drink? Try it, it's really refreshing - the vinegar mellows with the sugar and sparkling water.

Ingredients

500ml elderberries

500ml cider vinegar

25g shallots (finely chopped or minced)

A blade of mace

A 1cm cube ginger

1 teaspoonful cloves

1 teaspoonful black peppercorns

Sugar – see method for quantities

Method

Strip the berries from the stalks and rinse in water. Put them in a large jar with the vinegar and leave for 24 hours. Strain off the liquid without crushing the berries.

For the sauce - Transfer to a pan and add the shallots and spices and boil gently for five minutes.

Add the sugar. For each 500ml of liquid, use 200g sugar. Stir to dissolve the sugar, then pour through a sieve to remove the whole spices.

When cold, bottle and label.

For shrub - Transfer to a pan DO NOT ADD SHALLOT.

Add the spices and boil gently for five minutes.

Add the sugar. For each 500ml of liquid, use 500g sugar. Stir to dissolve the sugar, then pour through a sieve to remove the whole spices.

When cold bottle and label.

To serve, mix with sparking water.

Start with 1 part shrub to 6 parts sparkling water and adjust to taste. The syrup may also be mixed with still water or used in cocktails.

1950 – 1980

The Recipes

Sweets, Cakes & Biscuits

Soups, Stews & Savouries

Puddings

Extras

1950-1980

The History

The Background

Post war rationing was eventually phased out in the 1950s. Tea was still on ration until 1952. In 1953, rationing of sugar and eggs ended, and in 1954 all rationing finally ended when cheese and meats came off ration. This was followed by the years of plenty and with the catch phrase 'you've never had it so good.' The 50s and 60s were indeed a time of job rises and opportunities.

International travel, available to the man in the street in the 60s, expanded in the 70s. People came back from these trips wanting to try the exotic foods they had found abroad in their own kitchens.

The cold war became a grim reality because both sides had the power and technology for a nuclear holocaust, but equally both knew any war could not truly be won.

The Sixties also bought the space race to new heights. On July 20, 1969, Neil Alden Armstrong and Edwin Eugene 'Buzz' Aldrin, Jr. became the first humans to land on the moon through the Apollo 11 mission, fulfilling the American dream to place a man on the moon before the Russians. The words spoken by Neil Armstrong, 'That's one small step for man, one giant leap for mankind' made it into the history books for now and future generations to come.

The Kitchen

Affordable electric stoves became available in the 1950s. More than 60% of households had an electricity supply, and with the increased infrastructure for electricity, the cost of using an electric stove dropped dramatically. In the 1960s, automatic electric ovens allowed cooks to pre-time food.

Home cooks now also enjoyed the ease of using a counter-top stand mixer. These were initially available in the 1930s, but were now lighter and smaller. The hand-held mixer made its appearance too in the mid-1950s.

Already standard in Paris, non-stick coating became the norm for American household pans by the mid 1950s. New technology led to lighter pots and pans made of alternative materials, such as aluminum and stainless steel.

In 1947, the 'Radarange,' the first commercially available microwave, hit the American market, although they never really took off until the 1970s when prices were brought down to an acceptable level. Then, with improvements including a significant decrease in size (allowing for counter top placement), the microwave quickly became the standard for cooking, with microwaves outselling gas ranges by 1975.

In the UK, the Sixties saw the spread of that marvelous invention, Tupperware and the Tupperware party. Although Tupperware was invented by Earl Silas Tupper in the US in 1948, it didn't spread to Europe until 1960 when Mila Pond hosted a Tupperware party in Weybridge, England. Comedians loved to joke about Tupperware parties, but that just provided free publicity. By 1958, Mr. Tupper was able to sell his company for approximately sixteen million dollars and retire for life.

Melting Moments

Joan Neish

I love these biscuits - they were the main biscuit we ate as children. Sadly, we moaned that everyone else had bought biscuits while we had to make do with home baked ones!

Our mum used to make them with a mix of lard and margarine, but I use butter now.

You may have guessed, but this recipe doesn't come from an unknown kitchen. It's from a scribbled note my mum slipped into one of her cookery books.

Ingredients

150g butter

75g castor sugar

½ egg

½ teaspoon vanilla essence (this will vary with the type of vanilla essence you use)

150g self raising flour

Oats to roll

Method

Preheat oven to /375°F/190°C/ Gas 5.

Cream the butter and sugar until pale and creamy. Add the egg, vanilla and flour. Don't overmix - the texture will be soft.

You can make these biscuits to any size. A teaspoon of mixture will make small biscuits for children, but I always end making biscuits of all sizes.

Roll in oats and press slightly to flatten to about ½cm thick, then place on a greased baking tray.

Bake for 15 mins. They will be slightly soft when they come out of the oven. Put them straight onto a wire rack and by the time they have cooled, they will be crispy.

Harvo

G. R. Moore

Harvo is another name for malt loaf, a staple of 50s tea time and still popular.

Originally made by a company called Harvo that disappeared in the 70s, malt loaf has a sweet taste and a very chewy texture like very heavy, soft bread and - as its name suggests - contains malt extract.

Malt loaf is usually eaten sliced and with butter. This home version recipe didn't have fruit, however, so I have added sultanas. What's a malt loaf without sultanas?

Ingredients

250g brown flour

250g white flour

100g sugar

200g malt extract

150g treacle

250g sultanas

25g melted butter

1 teaspoon bicarbonate of soda

½ teaspoon salt

250ml milk

1 egg

Method

Preheat the oven to 180°C/350°F/Gas 4.

Line the base and ends of two greased 450g/1lb non-stick loaf tins with strips of baking parchment.

Mix everything together in the order it appears in the ingredient list and stir well. The mix should be of a soft dropping consistency.

Pour into the baking tins and bake for around 50 minutes,

Test with a skewer to make sure the center is cooked. Give it a few more minutes if not.

Carrots have been used in sweet cakes since the medieval period, during which time sweeteners were scarce and expensive, while carrots, which contain more sugar than any other vegetable besides the sugar beet, were much easier to come by and were used to make sweet desserts.

The origins of carrot cake are disputed. The popularity of carrot cake was probably revived in Britain because of rationing during the Second World War.

Carrot cakes first became commonly available in restaurants and cafeterias in the United States in the early 1960s. In 2005, the American-based Food Network listed carrot cake, with its cream-cheese icing, as number five of the top five 'fad foods' of the 1970s and it has stayed a favourite ever since.

I have updated this cake by using sunflower oil and by using a cream cheese filling rather than butter cream.

Carrot and Sultana Cake

Anon

Ingredients

250g carrots
110g sultanas/raisins
175g light muscovado sugar
125g sunflour oil
3 eggs, beaten
150g self-raising flour
1½ level teaspoons ground cinnamon
Good grating of nutmeg
1 level teaspoon bicarbonate of soda

Icing/filling

2 x 250g packs of cream cheese
125g melted butter
250g icing sugar
1 teaspoon vanilla extract

Method

Preheat the oven to 180°C/350°F/Gas 4.

Whisk together the sugar and oil, then whisk in the eggs.

Fold in the flour, cinnamon, nutmeg and bicarbonate of soda with a wooden spoon.

Stir in the carrots and raisins and combine thoroughly.

Pour into a 7 inch square greased and lined tin and bake for an hour or until well risen and firm to the touch. Test with a skewer - if the skewer emerges clean from the centre of the cake, it's baked.

When cooked, leave the cake in the tin for around 30 minutes before turning out onto a rack.

To make the icing, sieve the icing sugar into a bowl with the rest of the ingredients and mix well.

When the cake is cool, slice it in half and fill with the cream cheese icing. Replace the top half and spread that with the cream cheese icing too.

Undecorated, this cake can be frozen.

Soupe Au Pistou

Anon

Pistou, the Provençal cousin of pesto, is stirred into this summer vegetable soup just before serving.

The basics of the soup are the potato, courgettes and beans, but this is one of those recipes that can vary as much as you like in terms of the vegetables used. Broken spaghetti, rice or bread is sometimes added as well. Try it out and then make it your own.

Soup

1.5 litre water

1 tablespoon of olive oil

150g potatoes

150g onions

150g courgettes

150g aubergines

200g white haricot beans (a tin would be fine)

100g green beans

Salt and pepper to season

Pistou

4 crushed cloves garlic

4 cups basil

1 cup grated parmesan

¼ cup extra-virgin olive oil

1 teaspoon salt

1 plum tomato, cored

Method

Make the pistou:
Process basil, parmesan, olive oil, salt, garlic, and tomato in a food processor until finely ground, or attack with a pestle and mortar if you're feeling energetic. Season with salt and pepper, and set aside.

Prepare the vegetables:
Chop the potatoes, courgettes and aubergine into cubes, roughly chop the onions and chop the green beans into 1cm pieces.

Fry the onions in the oil, then add the rest of the vegetables and cook for five minutes.

Add the water and all of the fresh vegetables then season well. Cook for around 15–20 minutes.

Add the white haricot beans and cook for a further five minutes.

Add the pistou sauce and stir gently, then taste and season again if needed.

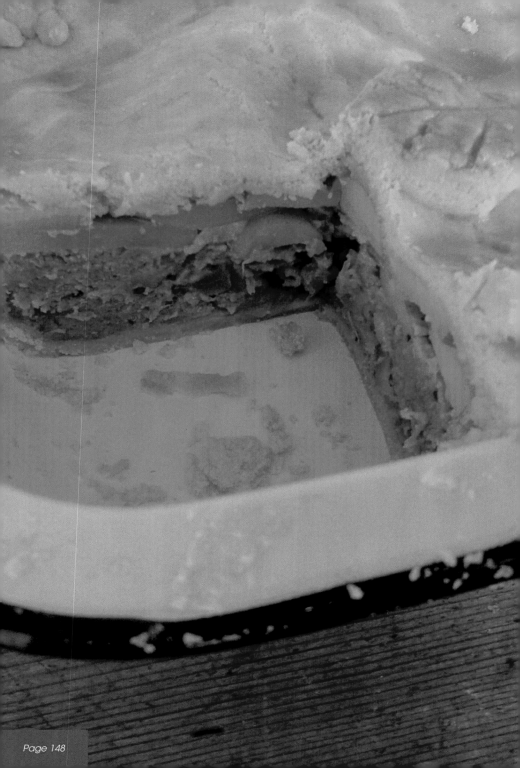

North Country Fidget Pie

G R Moore

Fidget Pie is a traditional English recipe for a pie served in the fields to workers busy bringing in the harvest. I can see why.

The name fidget (or fidgety) pie originates around Derbyshire and Shropshire, in the middle of the country. The origins of the odd-sounding name seem to have come from the fact that it originally was *fitched*, which means 'five sided' in Anglo-Saxon.

Generally, fidget pie includes apples and either bacon or ham, so this North Country version is quite unusual.

Pastry

250g plain flour

Pinch salt

175g margarine

1 egg yolk

1 tablespoon of cold water

Filling

1 finely chopped onion

250g sausagemeat

Pepper and salt

1 egg

250g raw potatoes

150g peas

Method

Make the pastry by popping the flour, salt and margarine in a processor, whizzing until the mix is like breadcrumbs then adding the egg yolk and the water to make a firm dough. Wrap in clingfilm and allow to rest in the fridge for half an hour or more.

Mix the chopped onion with the sausagemeat, season, and bind with the beaten egg.

If you are using frozen peas, defrost and drain well. if you are using fresh, cook gently then drain.

Roll out the pastry and use 2/3 to line the base of a pie dish.

Put in a layer of the sausagemeat mix, then a layer of potatoes, thinly sliced. Season well, then add the peas.

Use the remaining 1/3 of the pastry to form the lid, then glaze using beaten egg white.

Heat the oven to 190°C/375°F/ Gas 5. Bake for 30 minutes then reduce the heat to moderate – 180°C/350°F/Gas 4 - and cook for a further 15 minutes. Can be eaten hot or cold.

Bacon and Egg Pie

G R Moore

The English version of Quiche? There is some discussion about where this originated.

We Brits think it was a Victorian breakfast pie, but in New Zealand it is a popular household dish and it's common to come across it in menus of popular restaurants, so many people there claim that the pie probably originated in New Zealand. The jury is out on that one.

A very popular, cheap and filling meal, hot or cold.

Ingredients

500g of shortcrust pastry

300g bacon

1 medium onion (chopped)

5 eggs

30ml milk

1 tablespoon chopped parsley

100g peas

Salt and pepper

Method

Pre heat the oven to 200°C/400°F/Gas 6.

Cut the bacon into smallish pieces. Put the onion and bacon in a frying pan and cook on a medium heat until the onion is transparent, the bacon crisp and no liquid is left.

Roll ⅔ of the pastry and line a loose-bottomed flan tin about 8 inches diameter (20cm) and roughly 2 inches (5cm) deep. Roll the remaining ⅓ into a round to make the lid.

Lightly beat two of the eggs with 30ml milk and season; light on the salt but heavy on the pepper. Hard boil the remaining three eggs and chop roughly.

Place the bacon and onion mix in the pie, add a layer of chopped hard-boiled egg and the parsley, then pour on the egg mix.

Add a layer of peas and season again, then put on the pastry lid. Glaze with beaten egg. Bake for 10 minutes then reduce the heat to 180°C/350°F/Gas 4 and bake for another 30 minutes.

Beef Olives

G R Moore

The 1950s was a time of food experiment - I remember my mum's first spaghetti.

Beef Olives was typical of the new dishes. It is in fact a braised meat dish which had been popular in Scotland since the 1600s, but now had a revival with the arrival of the 'dinner party.'

Despite their name, they have nothing to do with olives the fruit; it is the beef parcels themselves that are the olives.

Ingredients

750g rump steak

50g breadcrumbs

25g suet

1 dessertspoonful parsley

Grated rind of a lemon

Salt & pepper

1 egg

600ml beef stock

1 medium onion (chopped)

1 tablespoon vegetable oil

Flour to coat

25g cornflour

Method

Preheat the oven to 150°C/325°F/Gas 3.

Cut the meat into four pieces and hammer them until they form thin slices and spread out.

Mix the breadcrumbs, suet, parsley, lemon rind and the egg with a good amount of seasoning. Put the mixture on the meat and roll it into a sausage, then tie with string or skewer.

Fry the onion in a little oil until cooked through and transparent, then transfer to a casserole dish.

Toss the beef olives in seasoned flour and fry them in the same pan as the onions until browned, then transfer them to the casserole.

Pour the beef stock into the pan and stir to gather up the flour and juices, then transfer to the casserole.

Bake in the oven for about two hours. If you want the sauce to be thicker, add the cornflour mixed with a little water.

Chicken Country Captain

G Watson

This dish comes from the southern states of America where there are hundreds of different versions and states vie as to where it originated. This version is very simple, Anglicised and very tasty. The chilli powder gives it a kick, so reduce it to your taste if needed.

Ingredients

4 x chicken portions

100g ghee or vegetable oil

A large sliced onion

1 teaspoon ground turmeric

1 teaspoon ground chilli

½ teaspoon salt

Method

Fry the onion in the ghee or oil depending on your preference until it is crispy and caramelised but not too dark.

Remove it from the pan and place on a plate with some kitchen roll to drain.

Add a little more oil to the pan if necessary then add the turmeric and chilli. Fry briefly then add the chicken.

Cook on a medium heat to ensure it is cooked through thoroughly, turning it regularly.

Cook for the first 15 minutes with a lid or cover on the pan then remove it to reduce any liquid. The cooking time will depend on the size of the chicken portions, but cook for about 30 minutes, then test.

I have also tried this using a tablespoon of the Curry Powder from page 56 and it works really well.

Serve with rice cooked your favourite way and with the onions on top.

Salade Fifi!

G Watson

I had to include this because I love the name, but as it turns out, the tarragon vinegar makes it a tasty option as well - especially for those, like me, who love raw mushrooms. The recipe recommends that this be eaten between the meal and the cheese course, but I say eat it when you want.

Salad

1 crisp cos or 2 little gem lettuces

½ cup sliced mushrooms

1 dessertspoon finely chopped chives and parsley

1 clove of garlic

Dressing

3 dessertspoons virgin olive oil

1 dessertspoon tarragon vinegar

Salt and pepper

Method

Rub the bowl with the garlic, then if you are a garlic lover, crush it and add to the dressing. Slice the lettuce and the mushrooms and place them in the bowl with the herbs. Cover and keep cool until needed. Make the dressing, but don't add it until just before serving.

Apple Snow

G R Moore

This recipe came from a time when people weren't worried about eating raw egg white, as the topping isn't cooked. If you are concerned about this, you can either make Italian meringue or used cooked meringue to top the dish.

As with most home dishes, there are a lot of versions of Apple Snow, most of which add the meringue to the apple pulp. This is rather like an apple trifle.

Ingredients

3–4 trifle sponges or left over cake

200g cooking apples, cored and peeled

Juice of a lemon

30 g sugar

100ml water

2 egg yolks

30g sugar

300ml milk

2 egg whites

1 tablespoon sugar

Method

The amount of sponge will depend on the size and shape of the dish you use.

Put the sponge in the bottom of a serving dish as for a trifle.

Cook the apple with the sugar, lemon juice and water until pulpy. This needs to be fairly liquid to soak the sponge.

Cover the sponge with the cooked apple.

Make the custard by mixing the egg yolks and sugar, heat the milk and add to the mix. Return to the pan and heat stirring constantly until thickened. Do not boil as the mix might curdle.

Pour the custard over the apple.

Whisk the egg whites, adding the sugar when the mix has thickened. Continue whisking until it forms small peaks.

Alternatively, you can use the easy cook version by using tinned custard and crumbling bought meringue over the top - much quicker.

Arabella's Cheesecake

Anon

Although there are recipes for cheesecake or curd cheesecake which date back hundreds of years, the modern cooked cheesecake was a favourite in the 1960's when 'dinner parties' started to become more popular for the average person. Prompted mainly by the new convenience appliances and the availability of more interesting ingredients, people were making more of a social thing of dinner. Absolutely delicious with tart summer fruits.

Base

250g digestive biscuits

¼ teaspoon nutmeg

125g melted butter

¼ teaspoon cinnamon

Filling

100g Philadelphia cheese

1 teaspoon vanilla essence

4 eggs

250ml carton cottage cheese

175g castor sugar

Topping

450 ml sour cream

1 ½ tablespoons castor sugar

¼ teaspoon vanilla essence

Method

Preheat the oven to 180°C/350°F/Gas 4.

Reduce biscuits to crumbs, add the butter and spices and use them to line a flan tin 8 inches diameter (20cm) and about 2 inches (5cm) deep

Mash together the cheese, sugar and vanilla. When blended, add the eggs one at a time, beating until each one is completely incorporated before adding the next. When it is a smooth mixture, tip it into the tin onto the biscuit base. Bake for 25–30 minutes until it is golden brown.

Stir the topping ingredients until smooth, then when the cheesecake is cool, tip the topping over it. Raise the oven temperature to 200°C/400°F/Gas 6 then return to the oven for 5-6 minutes, just enough for the topping to set.

Chill. You can make this 2-3 days before serving, stored in the fridge. It also freezes well.

The Queen's Recipe Barley Water

Anon

Barley water - the Wimbledon favourite. Written down as *The Queen's Barley Water* – I wonder which queen?

Good for all sorts of things according to old wives, from slowing down wrinkles to use as a restorative. I just like the taste and the addition of honey rather than sugar makes this version particularly good.

Ingredients

12g barley

3 litres of boiling water

2 lemons

6 oranges

Honey to sweeten

Method

Put the barley in a large saucepan, add the boiling water and simmer over a low heat with the lid on for one hour.

Squeeze the fruit and keep the juice.

Strain the water from the barley into a bowl, adding the rinds of one lemon and three oranges. Allow to stand until cold.

Strain off the rinds, add the orange and lemon juice and the honey to taste.

Stored in the fridge, this will keep for about a week.

Vin D'Oranges

Anon

This veritable French recipe packs quite a punch.

Eau de Vie is a French clear, colorless fruit brandy that is produced by means of fermentation and double distillation and it can also be made from grapes. The fruit flavour is typically very light. If you can't find Eau de Vie, Grappa or Schnapps could be used.

I have tried this with both red and white wine. Let's just say there is only some of the white wine version left.

Ingredients

1 litre of good wine

1 litre of eau de vie

22 sugar lumps

18 heads of chamomile

30g of zest of orange (dried)

1 whole lemon, quartered

Method

Add all of the ingredients to an airtight container. Leave to soak for 1 month, then filter and store in clean bottles.

1980 – 2000

The Background

The beginning of the 1980s continued the unrest of the late 1970s. In 1981, the Welsh group 'Women for Life on Earth' arrived at Greenham Common where they set up a Peace Camp just outside the fence of Greenham Common RAF Air Base in protest against the decision to store nuclear missiles there. The site wasn't closed until 2000.

This period saw huge contradictions in lifestyles. Alongside real hardship through lost jobs, there was the rise and fall of the 'yuppy' era, Thatcher's generation of young city workers with large amounts of disposable income. One of the ways they demonstrated this was through eating and drinking - this was a time of specialist cooking ingredients and flashy restaurants, and of spending enormous sums on wine and food. So the food scene was a mix of economy and lavish dining.

Famine in Ethiopia was shown to the world on our television screens in 1984-1985 and the pain and suffering caused the western world to find new ways to help, including the Live Aid concert where many of the most popular stars contributed their time and performed for free in cities throughout the world. This has to be one of the most successful campaigns ever to create awareness and raise much-needed funds by those who have the power to draw TV audiences around the globe.

Argentina invaded and occupied the Falkland islands in 1982 but was subsequently defeated by the United Kingdom.

In the early 90s, many in the UK were affected by the boom in house prices coming to an end which left many with negative equity. In 1990, the inflation rate was over 10%.

The rise in the number of vegetarians in the 80s and 90s escalated as environmental issues dominated the headlines and were for a time foregrounded in politics. In 1988, Edwina Curry started a scare over salmonella in eggs and in the mid-1990s, health concerns were raised following the 'Mad Cow Disease' (BSE) scare.

The Recipes

Sweets, Cakes & Biscuits

Soups, Stews & Savouries

Puddings

Pickles & Preserves

Extras

Drinks

By the 1990's we were all being urged to go back to the land, to grow and cook our own food rather than rely on the processed foods that had become so common. This provided the perfect gap for a young Hugh Fearnley-Whittingstall to leap onto our screens from River Cottage and home-grown has never looked back.

One of the biggest changes during this time was – you've guessed it – the internet. The 1980s saw the development of the modern internet. It was released to the public in July 1991 and by approximately 1995 became widely known, beginning the ongoing worldwide boom of internet use.

The Kitchen

Although they had always been around, celebrity chefs were now well on their way up, proliferating at a rate of knots.

Some have stood the test of time – Jamie Oliver, Nigella Lawson, Madhur Jaffrey and Delia Smith, to name but a few. Celebrity chefs and television made certain foods popular, in what has since been termed the 'Delia effect'.

The Delia effect caused a nationwide liquid glucose shortage in 1990 when she listed it in a recipe for *truffletorte*. In 1994 there was a lime and coriander crisis when they were key ingredients in her recipe book **Summer Collection** and in 1995 there was a cranberry famine after the little-known berries were named as her 'ingredient of the year' and pictured on the cover of **Winter Collection**.

The huge numbers of available cookery books from celebrity chefs and food magazines meant that people didn't write down as many recipes. They tended to cut out recipes from magazines, buy a book or - later in the 1990s - get recipes from the internet. The 'unknown kitchen' becomes harder to find now.

Cooking habits changed. Some people stopped cooking altogether as ready meals became ever more available and microwaves became more sophisticated. Meanwhile the trend to 'Grow and Cook Your Own' started to take hold and cooking in the nineties moved towards using fewer and fresher local ingredients.

This was also reflected in the resurgence of the AGA range. Always popular, it now became the 'must-have' kitchen item.

Honey Truffles

Anon

I'm surprised that I found fewer recipes for sweets than I expected. These lovely truffles just hit the spot though.

Ingredients

400g dark chocolate (72% solids)

25g unsalted butter

20g clear honey

200g double cream

Approx. 30g cocoa powder

Method

Finely chop or grate 250g of the chocolate into a bowl and add the honey and butter.

Put the cream into a small saucepan and bring just to the boil.

Pour the cream over the chocolate and honey mix whisking until it is smooth. Don't whisk too quickly, as you don't want to cause air bubbles.

Cool a little, then pop in the fridge to set for around half an hour. To cool the mix down quickly, pour it into a flat pan or a rimmed baking sheet and press clingfilm on top of the chocolate, to prevent a skin from forming.

Melt the remaining chocolate in a bain-marie or in a bowl over simmering water.

Take small scoops of the truffle mix and pop into the melted chocolate to coat, then place them on a cold plate to set. I found it easier to make square ones and I think they look nicer.

Roll them in the cocoa powder to finish.

Pumpkin Soup With Chilli & Black Beans

(Anon)

The nineties saw the rise of pumpkins & squashes, especially roasted or in soup.

These vegetables which had previously been not only ignored but actually disliked became very popular when reintroduced by TV chefs.

Here is a nice version with chillies and beans.

Ingredients

60ml olive oil

3 cloves garlic

2 small red chillis (deseeded)

1.5 kg pumpkin (peeled and deseeded)

2 medium onions (chopped)

200g potatoes (diced)

Juice of 1 large lemon

Grated nutmeg to taste

1 litres hot vegetable stock

200g can black beans (drained)

10g butter

To serve

30g fresh coriander (roughly chopped)

100 g crème fraiche

200g greek yoghurt

Method

Chop the pumpkin and potatoes into cubes of about 1cm. Add the oil to a large pan, fry the onions until softened.

Add all of the soup ingredients except the beans.

Simmer for about 15-20 minutes until the pumpkin and potatoes are soft

Whizz in a blender until smooth and return to the pan. Add the black beans - I found that mashing them a little first gives a better texture. Stir in the butter.

To serve, add the chopped coriander.

Mix together the crème fraiche and yoghurt and swirl in or put in a side dish so that people can help themselves.

Hil's Soup

(Anon)

In the nineties, recipes were becoming fresher and more emphasis was put on making the most of flavours with fewer ingredients.

This is a deceptively plain soup. The fennel and rosemary give it a really delicious flavour. Having tried it out for this book, I now make it regularly.

Do use good quality tinned tomatoes rather than fresh, as it seems to give a better flavour.

Ingredients

200g carrots

2 sticks celery

1 onion (chopped)

3 cloves garlic (big fat ones)

1 sprig rosemary

½ tin chopped tomatoes

½ teaspoon fennel seeds

2 bay leaves

1 litre vegetable stock

A handful of chopped parsley

1 tablespoon olive oil

Salt & pepper

Method

Heat 4 tablespoons of oil in a large pan, add the onion and cook slowly. When soft, add the chopped celery and garlic.

Chop the carrots and celery into small cubes, about ½ cm, and add to the pan. Cook until tender, then add the tomatoes.

Remove the rosemary leaves from the stem, chop them finely then add to the pan with the fennel seeds and bay leaves and cook for 2 minutes.

Add the stock, then bring to boil and simmer for 15 minutes or until the vegetables are cooked, but with just a little bite.

Season with salt & pepper and add parsley at the end.

This is a deceptively plain soup...

Mary's Greek Fish

Anon

This dish reflects the move toward simpler food freshly made. With a few ingredients, you can produce delicious results. This author really loved her fresh summer dishes.

Like a lot of recipes in this period, it also reflects the Brits' growing love of Mediterranean food, bringing back memories of holidays.

Ingredients

1 large tin of peeled tomatoes

Bream, fresh haddock or turbot for 4

Large handful of fresh parsley and oregano

2 large onions

1 clove of chopped garlic

½ cup olive oil

Salt and pepper

Method

Preheat the oven to 180°C/350°F/Gas 4.

Place filleted fish in a flat oven dish with a lid.

Fry the finely-chopped onions in olive oil very gently until transparent. Add the garlic and continue cooking for a few more minutes

Add the tomatoes. When mushy, add the chopped herbs, salt and pepper to taste. Pour the mixture over the fish and bake in the oven for around 45 minutes.

This doesn't need anything with it apart from some crusty bread to soak up the last juices.

This author really loved her fresh summer food.

Tabbouli

Anon

Traditionally served as part of a mezze in the Arab world, tabbouleh has become a popular ethnic vegetarian food in the West, where it is often spelled *tabbouli*.

Tabbouli and its cousin cous cous saved us from the food crime from the 60s and 70s that was rice salad, tasteless and dotted with raw peppers and tinned sweetcorn.

Ingredients

1 cup of cracked bulgar wheat

Boiling water

2 big bunches of chopped parsley

1 small red onion, finely chopped

Juice of 3 lemons

Three slices of lemon, chopped small

¼ teaspoon of ground allspice

4 large chopped tomatoes

4 tablespoons of virgin olive oil

Salt & pepper to taste

Method

Wash the bulgar wheat and drain. Cover in boiling water and leave to soak until tender. Add more water if required - the age of the bulgar wheat changes the amount of water needed.

Add the rest of the ingredients and mix thoroughly with a fork

Adjust the seasoning to taste.

Colcannon

Anon

The recipe is written as *My Colcannon*, which says it all. Although traditionally Colcannon has potato and cabbage as the main ingredients, this is a dish for which everyone had their own version. This recipe includes carrots and turnips.

Ingredients

1 cabbage

4–6 potatoes

4–6 young carrots

4 6 young turnips

Salt & freshly ground black pepper

150ml single cream

2 egg yolks

50g butter

Fresh grated cheese

Method

Cook cabbage and potatoes until tender.

Peel and slice carrots and turnips in thin strips and blanch them in sufficient water to cover.

Add butter and 4 tablespoons of water to pan, cover and simmer until veg are tender. Season to taste.

Chop cabbage finely and mash potatoes until smooth. Add cream, egg yolks, additional butter and pepper & salt to taste.

Spread half of the cabbage/potato mixture in the bottom of a well-buttered oven proof dish. Arrange alternate strips of carrots and turnips down the centre.

Cover with remaining cabbage/potato mixture and Sprinkle with fresh breadcrumbs.

Top with grated cheese, and dot with butter.

Cook in an oven at 190°C/375°F/ Gas 5 for 30 minutes or until golden brown.

Jacqueline Boeuf Au Vin
Anon

I'm assuming that Jacqueline is a friend, as I can't find a dish of this name.

This is a great alternative to a Sunday roast.

Ingredients

1.5kg piece of lean topside near end muscle

200g sliced shallots

200g sliced carrots

A few sprigs of thyme

A small bunch of parsley

1 bottle of fruity red wine

1 tablespoon cornflour

1 oz butter

A good glug of brandy

Method

Soak the meat in the wine for 24hrs or at least overnight with the parsley, shallots and thyme. if the meat isn't covered by the wine, turn it a few times.

Heat a frying pan or flameproof casserole, add the brandy and butter and flambé the meat, then brown it on all sides.

Place the meat in an ovenproof casserole dish, add the carrots and marinade and season well.

Cook for 2 hours, turning 2 or 3 times. Cook with the lid on, but allow time for the wine to reduce.

If you want the sauce to be thicker, add the cornflour mixed with a little water.

A great alternative to a Sunday roast.

Tarte Aux Pizza à La Jacqueline

Anon

Good old Jacqueline again. This recipe for Pizza Tart is a lovely combination of pizza flavours in a rich pastry flan, making it a bit lighter than pizza base. This pastry is rich and a bit fragile when you roll it out.

Pastry case

250g plain flour

125g butter

A pinch of salt

1 egg

1 tablespoon of olive oil

1 tablespoon of cold water

Filling

250g chopped onion

250g tomatoes

50g tin of anchovy fillets

30g Gruyère cheese (or similar)

Few sprigs of chopped oregano

Method

Mix the flour and butter with fingertips till all crumbly, add a pinch of salt, one egg, then the oil and cold water.

Make quickly into a ball - don't overwork. Wrap iin clingfilm and put in the fridge to rest.

Preheat the oven to 190°C/400°F/Gas 5.

Roll out the pastry and line a 1″ deep flan dish. Don't roll too thinly.

Blind bake the flan case for around 20 minutes, then paint the bottom with beaten egg and cook for another five minutes.

Filling

Put the onions and oil in a frying pan and soften them, but don't brown.

After a few minutes, add the tomatoes cut into slices. You can also use cherry tomatoes halved, which look pretty in the flan.

When nearly cooked but not mushy, fill the flan case, grate the Gruyère cheese over it and criss-cross with the anchovy fillets.

Bake for around 25 - 30 minutes until the cheese has melted.

Poached Chicken and Salsa Verde

Anon

During the 1990s, flat-leaved parsley became the 'in' herb. Now nobody was going to cook with curly parsley!

For the Chicken

6 skinless pieces of chicken or whole chicken

150ml white wine

1 unpeeled onion, coarsely chopped

2 cloves garlic

1 unpeeled carrot

Sprig rosemary, sage or thyme

For the Salsa Verde

75g anchovy fillets

4 cloves garlic, peeled

3 level tablespoons capers, well rinsed

3 tablespoons lemon juice or vinegar

3 level tablespoons Dijon mustard

20g flat-leaved parsley, leaves only

125g fresh basil

12 tablespoons virgin olive oil

Freshly ground pepper

Method

Place the chicken in a large saucepan. Add wine, veg, herbs, garlic and enough water to cover. Bring to the boil, then simmer for 20 minutes in barely-moving water until just cooked.

Meanwhile, chop the anchovy, garlic, capers, vinegar, mustard in a food processor. Add the herbs then pulse whilst drizzling in the oil.

Season to taste with the pepper - the anchovies will probably give enough salt. If you want a chunkier texture, do this by hand.

Remove the chicken pieces from the pan. Serve warm or cold with the salsa and salad.

Salade Pêcheur

Mike

Fresh seafood freshly cooked. If you want a real trip down memory lane to the South of France, cook this – then follow it with the Peaches in Wine on page 190.

Method

600g mussels

250g haddock fillet (or mackerel)

100ml malt vinegar

250g new potatoes

100g shallots (finely chopped)

1 large clove of garlic (smashed)

150g cooked french beans (or a small tin)

French dressing

Seasoning

Chervil

Method

Marinate the fish overnight in vinegar. Cook the potatoes.

Mussels must be thoroughly cleaned and rinsed several times before cooking. Once the mussels have been thoroughly cleaned, remove and discard any shells that are open or broken and that do not close when tapped.

Cook the mussels in a large pan with a little water or white wine. Mussels only need to be steamed in a tiny amount of liquid - when they open up during cooking, they release their own liquid, which makes a tasty broth or sauce. Shell the mussels, reserving a few for decoration. Place them in a large salad bowl.

Add the cockles, the fish, the potatoes (and I quote, 'chopped roughly and butchly'), the shallot, garlic, beans and dressing. Add seasoning and chopped chervil. Toss.

Decorate with the 6 mussels you should have left unshelled.

Great served just with garlic bread (heavy on the garlic) some crunchy samphire and a glass of wine.

Peaches in Wine

Anon

Summertime and the living is easy... Peaches are symbolic of a French summer. In the Eighties, good French wine became cheap enough that we could afford to cook with it. This recipe comes as a reminder of warm evenings sipping wine by the Mediterranean.

Ingredients

50g castor sugar

150ml hot water

½ teaspoon ground cinnamon

150ml red wine

4 x peaches

Juice of ½ lemon

Grated peel from ½ orange and ½ lemon

Method

Preheat the oven to 180°C/350°F/Gas 4.

Cut the peaches in half and remove the stone, then put them face-down in a flat dish with a lid. Add the sugar, water and cinnamon and simmer for 15 mins. If you don't have a dish with a lid, cover it with foil.

Peel the peaches and return to the dish, add the wine, lemon juice and grated orange and lemon peel and cook gently uncovered for 15 minutes. When cooked, pour off the liquid and reduce to a syrup.

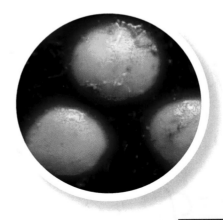

Crema Catalan

Chloe

Crema Catalan (or Catalana to give it its proper Spanish name) is like a crème brûlée only lighter, as it is made with milk rather than cream.

Apparently there is a dispute between Spain and France about which came first: crema Catalana or crème brûlée. Each side claims that the other stole the original and changed the name. In fact, many regions lay claim to the origin of the dessert.

Wherever it originated, enjoy and let it dissolve in your mouth! It is a great dessert for Spring, since it is also called Crema de Sant Josep, or St. Joseph's cream, traditionally prepared on March 19th, St. Joseph's Day, the Spanish equivalent of Father's Day.

Ingredients

500ml milk

4 egg yolks

75g of sugar plus extra to caramelise

Zest of a lemon

Method

In a medium saucepan, bring the milk and lemon zest to a boil, then reduce the heat to low and simmer for 3 minutes to infuse the flavour.

In a large bowl, whisk the egg yolks with the sugar until pale and fluffy. Add the cornflour and whisk until thoroughly combined.

Pass through a sieve to remove the lemon zest from the milk. Gradually add the milk to the egg yolk mixture, stirring well, then return the mixture to the saucepan and heat over a medium heat, stirring continuously.

When the mix has thickened to a consistency that will cover the back of the spoon, divide the custard between four ramekins and smooth the tops.

Cool the custards slightly, then cover the ramekins with cling film and refrigerate them until the custard is cold - at least 8 or up to 24 hrs.

To serve, sprinkle each ramekin evenly with a teaspoon of sugar. The Spanish method of caramelising is with an iron device. Failing that, use a kitchen torch or put under a hot grill to caramelise the sugar until browned and crusty. Serve immediately.

Gingernuts & Whipped Cream

(Anon)

I remember sitting through quite a few dinner parties when this was the pudding, around the time life became 'too short to stuff mushrooms.' It did the rounds for a short time before going out of fashion. Heavy on the cream, so don't serve to anyone on a diet!

Ingredients

2 packets of ginger nuts
600ml double cream
Sherry, brandy or ginger wine
20g candied ginger, chopped

Method

Whip the cream until solid then take the biscuits one by one, dip into the sherry and add a blob of cream.

Carry on like this, wedging the biscuits together with the cream. Don't be tempted to soak all the biscuits beforehand as they will just disintegrate

You can use sherry, brandy or ginger wine - or mix ginger wine and sherry.

Decorate the top with candied ginger.

Store in the fridge until used, this will keep for a few days in the fridge.

Mary's Quince Jelly

Anon

In the nineties, it started to become fashionable to make jams, jellies and chutneys again. There was a move towards home-made, home-grown food, giving rise to TV programmes like *The River Cottage*.

Previously unfashionable fruits like quinces and meddlars became fashionable in the competition to show who was eating or cooking with the most unusual ingredients.

Ingredients

1 ½ kg quinces

3 large cooking apples

Sugar

Method

Rinse and chop the fruit.

In a pan of water, just cover the fruit and cook until it becomes a pulp.

Tip into muslin & allow to drip - preferably overnight, but for at least two hours.

Measure the liquid and transfer to a pan. For each pint of liquid, add 500g sugar.

Bring to the boil gently to dissolve the sugar then bring to a rolling boil. Cook, keeping well skimmed and removing any scum.

After 15 minutes, test for setting using a saucer that has been chilled in the fridge. Put a small blob on the saucer and leave to cool slightly. Gently push your fingertips through it - the surface will wrinkle if the jam is at setting point.

Remove the pan from the heat while testing - if the jelly overboils, it will become syrupy and will never set.

Go on testing every few minutes so that you don't overcook it. Jellies are better slightly loose than too thick.

Bottle in clean warmed jars and label.

Pesto

Anon

Pesto really came into its own in the 1980s and thankfully hasn't left.

Here someone has discovered the fabulous stuff, and the Magimix. *Magimix* was the original pioneer of the food processor over 35 years ago in Burgundy, France, by French catering company salesman, Pierre Verdan.

He observed the vast amount of time his clients spent in the kitchen chopping, shredding and mixing. He felt there must be an easier way - so he produced a simple but effective solution, a bowl with a revolving blade in the base. Magimix has used this first model and evolved this down the years to the modern versions of today.

The thing I like about this recipe is the haphazard approach to measurement, which I think is the secret to good pesto. I haven't changed the recipe or method as I think it speaks for itself.

Ingredients

2 large packs pine nuts – roasted under the grill slightly and chopped lightly in the magi mix

Chunk of parmesan chopped up finely in magi mix

3 ENORMOUS cups of basil

1 bulb of garlic chopped and mashed

500mls olive oil

Method

Put basil in magi mix and blend until saucy.

Then add chopped parmesan, pinenuts, garlic and a bit of salt.

Then start pouring the oil in while the whizz is whizzing.

Et viola (or the Italian equivalent.)

Elderflower Cordial

Clarice

Ah, the taste of spring and summer. I look forward to this every year and try to make enough to last through the summer and a little extra. It doesn't always work. This recipe was written down by a friend's mother and is absolutely the best I have found. Elderflowers are in season at around the end of May, so be ready.

Ingredients

24 – 32 large elderflower heads

4 lemon (thickly sliced)

50g citric acid

2 kg granulated sugar

Method

Cut off all the flowers and discard the stems.

Put the flowers, citric acid, lemons and sugar into a large plastic or glass bowl.

Add a kettleful of boiling water. Stir well with a plastic or wooden spoon, until the sugar has dissolved then cover with clingfilm, leaving the handle of the spoon sticking out.

Stir three times a day for 4 – 5 days without removing the spoon.

Strain the mix through muslin and bottle in clean bottles and label.

Add water to taste when you serve. This can be frozen if you put it in plastic bottles. Not only does it taste lovely as a cool drink but it makes great elderflower sorbet.

Oh, and it is really delicious used to cook with gooseberries, that classic partnership.

References

And further reading

Delia Effect
http://www.thefreelibrary.com
Delia+factor%3B+Forget+abo
ut+
sophisticated+marketing+strat
egies+
.+....-a060614024

Cream Flummery history
http://www.foodsofengland.
co.uk
/flummery.htm

A Heritage of British Cookery
Maggie Black (Charles Letts &
Co, 1977)

Grains of Paradise info
http://www.gourmetsleuth.
com/
Dictionary/G/Grains-of-
paradise-5980.aspx

Salad Cream during rationing
http://pubs.rsc.org/en/
Content/ArticleLanding/1945/
AN/an9457000306#!divAbstract

Consider the Fork
Bee Wilson (Particular Books
2012)

A Century of British Cooking
Marguerite Patten (Grub Street
Press 1999)

**Licks, Sticks and Bricks:
A History of Ice Cream**
Pim Reinders (Unilever 1999)

Moveable Feasts
Arnold Palmer (Oxford
University Press, 1952)

The recipes in this book are not vegetarian but if, like me, you care where your food comes from. Here are some organisations who work to make sure that the ingredients you use have the least negative impact on animals, people and the environment.

Compassion in World Farming

http://www.ciwf.org.uk/

CIWF campaigns peacefully to end all cruel factory farming practices. They believe that the biggest cause of cruelty on the planet deserves a focused, specialised approach and so work on farm animal welfare.

Fair Trade Foundation

http://www.fairtrade.org.uk/

The Fairtrade Foundation is the independent non-profit organisation that licenses use of the FAIRTRADE Mark on products in the UK in accordance with internationally agreed Fairtrade standards.

The Soil Association

http://www.soilassociation.org/

The Soil Association are the UK's leading membership charity campaigning for healthy, humane and sustainable food, farming and land use.

Marine Stewardship Council

http://www.msc.org/

The MSC runs an exciting and ambitious program, working with partners to transform the world's seafood markets and promote sustainable fishing practices.

A percentage of the profits from this book go to Compassion in World Farming

About Rita Godfrey

And Refried Books

Rita is based in Arundel, Sussex, in a house with a long thin garden, a small kitchen and two cats. She shares an allotment with her partner Terry, which takes up a lot of her spare time.

A while ago she decided to make a change and take the step to make a living out of something she really enjoys by setting up Refried Books, an online shop for used, vintage and antiquarian books about cooking and gardening - in fact, everything to do with food, cooking, wine and growing things.

Rita declined a photo but instead suggested a picture of her teapot, saying, 'If I was a teapot this would be me.'

Refried Books
www.refriedbooks.co.uk

Notes From Your Kitchen